THE LAST OF THE RADICALS

JOSIAH WEDGWOOD, M.P.

THE LAST OF THE RADICALS

JOSIAH WEDGWOOD, M.P.

by

C. V. WEDGWOOD

JONATHAN CAPE
THIRTY BEDFORD SQUARE LONDON

FIRST PUBLISHED 1951
REISSUED 1974

JONATHAN CAPE LTD, 30 BEDFORD SQUARE, LONDON WCI

ISBN 0 224 01097 2

PRINTED IN GREAT BRITAIN BY
LOWE & BRYDONE (PRINTERS) LTD, THETFORD, NORFOLK

CONTENTS

INTRODUCTION

JOSIAH CLEMENT WEDGWOOD sat in Parliament for thirty-seven years, for thirty-five of them in the House of Commons representing Newcastle-under-Lyme, and for two years in the House of Lords, a body to which he had once in his youth referred as a 'fossilized mummy'. He began as a Liberal, later joined the Labour party, but was essentially an independent. By nature an individualist rather than a party man, he was consistent even in his inconsistencies. His guiding principles never altered: he hated oppression and believed, with crusading fervour, that only in an atmosphere of freedom can man develop as a responsible political being. In the education of men to understand what they owed to themselves and to each other he saw the solution of all problems.

His was not a career of unmitigated success. Sometimes he doubted whether there had been success at all. 'It seems that I have failed,' he wrote in his *Memoirs of a Fighting Life*, 'but I cannot see how, when, or where.' His significance was of character, rather than of achievement. He came to stand for an independent attitude in politics the value of which in our time has increased with its rarity. It is not the attitude which makes for ministerial or party success; he lacked some of the qualities and all the failings which make for a career within the framework of party politics.

Justice and the integrity of the individual came first with him, and he conceived of politics not as the art of the possible but as an aspiration towards the impossible. If a thing seemed right to him, he liked it all the better for being inexpedient.

9

Pleased with the danger, when the waves went high
He sought the storms;

but, unlike Achitophel in this, as in other ways, he
did not seek danger 'to boast his wit'. He sought it
because it was his delight to pit men against fate in a
conflict whose inequality he recognized. He lost
interest in a winning cause, for it no longer needed
him.

This characteristic partly explains the variation of
his interests — Freedom for India, the Russian Revolution, Conscientious Objectors, Refugees from Fascism,
the Jews. It was also the reason why he subscribed
throughout his life consistently to only one political
doctrine — the Taxation of Land Values as advocated
by Henry George. As a political doctrine Georgian
socialism has been submerged by the Marxist school.
He believed in it defiantly to the end and when asked
his politics by foreign journalists seeking information or
earnest young people at tea on the Terrace, he would
cause bewilderment by announcing himself to be a
Single-taxer, a party of which they had not heard.
For him it remained always 'the good old cause'.

His deepest faith was neither in a theory nor a cause.
He strove to preserve, in politics and through politics,
a certain quality of the human soul, a defiant integrity,
a Protestantism which does not cease to protest. In
the family vocabulary there were a number of sayings
remembered and quoted, or misquoted, from the
history books on which he and his brothers had been
reared. Among these was one which came frequently
to his lips. Sir Ralph Percy, dying in one of the
battles of the Wars of the Roses, is supposed to have
uttered the cryptic boast: 'I have saved the bird in
my bosom.' The precise meaning is uncertain, but

frequent quotation had endowed it with significance; the bird was — what? The captive soul striving upward? Loyalty? Truth? Freedom? All these things perhaps. Quoting the words in a letter to one of his daughters towards the end of his life, Josiah added: 'A very pretty sentiment which you may inscribe on my tomb — for I have kept very little else.' It was enough to keep and more than most men do.

London 1951   C.V.W.

Postscript 1974

The text of this biography remains as I wrote it when the memory of my uncle, Josiah Clement Wedgwood, was fresh in my mind. At that time the controversies in which he was involved, the events in which he played his part and the causes for which he fought were still too near to be seen in historical perspective. But it seemed to me when I looked at this book after an interval of more than twenty years, that it contained immediate impressions more vivid than long-term memories can ever be. What I had tried to write was essentially a personal memoir, not a political history. I sought to capture, before it faded, an impression of his strong, impulsive, generous personality and his integrity of purpose. While he lived he was a staunch friend to many in distress, a hope and an inspiration to those who worked with him and shared his love of liberty. Friendships and personal memories pass with the passing of time; but the inspiration of a strong personality survives in time and history and can be carried over to fresh causes and younger generations.

C.V.W.

THE LAST OF THE RADICALS

JOSIAH WEDGWOOD, M.P.

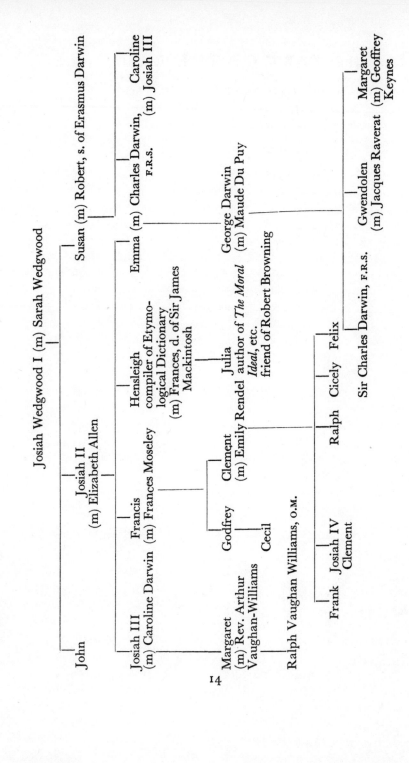

Josiah Wedgwood I (m) Sarah Wedgwood

John

Susan (m) Robert, s. of Erasmus Darwin

Josiah II
(m) Elizabeth Allen

Caroline
(m) Josiah III

Emma (m) Charles Darwin,
F.R.S.

Josiah III
(m) Caroline Darwin

Francis (m) Frances Moseley

Hensleigh
compiler of Etymo-
logical Dictionary
(m) Frances, d. of Sir James
Mackintosh

George Darwin
(m) Maude Du Puy

Margaret
(m) Rev. Arthur
Vaughan-Williams

Godfrey

Cecil

Clement
(m) Emily Rendel

Julia
author of *The Moral
Ideal*, etc.
friend of Robert Browning

Gwendolen
(m) Jacques Raverat

Margaret
(m) Geoffrey
Keynes

Ralph Vaughan Williams, O.M.

Frank   Josiah IV
Clement

Ralph   Cicely   Felix

Sir Charles Darwin, F.R.S.

CHAPTER I

FAMILY BACKGROUND

T HE Wedgwood family resembles many others
recorded in the social history of England. They
were a healthy yeoman stock first called by name
in Staffordshire towards the end of the fifteenth
century. Some of the branches of this hardy country
tree raised themselves, temporarily at least, into the
sphere of the gentry and obtained a coat of arms. In
the main, the family continued closer to the earth,
engaged, as the centuries unfolded, in small trading
and above all in the Staffordshire industry of pots.
Josiah Wedgwood I — 'old Josiah' to his many and
grateful descendants — had four generations of master-
potters behind him, all practitioners of a traditional,
domestic industry in which sons were apprenticed to
fathers and younger to elder brothers. This last was
the lot of Josiah I, a thirteenth child, whose father
died when he was still a boy.

Josiah set up on his own in 1759 and in the next thirty-
five years revolutionized the manufacture of pottery
and accumulated a fortune of half a million pounds.
His wife, Sarah, a cousin, the daughter of Richard
Wedgwood, cheesemonger, who was also a Unitarian
preacher, had given him a numerous family. The
painter Stubbs drew their likenesses in return for the
pains Wedgwood had taken to produce large earthen-
ware plaques for his experiments in painting on
pottery. There they all are, Josiah and Sarah, seated
under a tree on the lawn of their country residence,
with their elder children grouped on their ponies, and
the two babies sporting in a go-cart. It is a picture solid

as the world it presents: a prosperous middle-class family enjoying an afternoon of well-merited leisure.

After one or two changes and partnerships, the firm, with its headquarters at the Etruria Works, had been stabilized under the name of Josiah Wedgwood and Sons. Of these sons John, the volatile and cherished heir, broke away from the potbank, embraced banking and horticulture, and would have liked to embrace the landed gentry. He was one of the founders of the Royal Horticultural Society. Later he was unlucky with his speculations. His family, however, rescued him, by joint subscription, from imminent bankruptcy and set him up on a small but respectable estate near Bath. His sons went into the Church and the Guards.

The second son, Josiah, bearing the name which is usually bestowed on cadets, succeeded his father as head of the firm. The second Josiah, a reserved and upright man who showed his disapproval of the Prince Regent's morals by refusing to take him over the Works, had a more difficult time to negotiate than his father. Money troubles darken these years of family history; not that the frugal Wedgwoods were ever seriously embarrassed, but the profits from china diminished in the Napoleonic wars, and Josiah II could not always meet calls on his charity as he would have wished. When prosperous, he supported generously not only his poorer relations, but poets, inventors and men of learning in want; the net of his constructive charity was cast wide. But in bad times he had to retrench and the subsidy he paid to his friend Samuel Taylor Coleridge, for instance, was stopped in the year 1812. It has been sometimes stated that Josiah cut off supplies because he disapproved of Coleridge's opium-smoking. The reason was a simpler one; Josiah's puritanism was not of a kind to affect his charity while he had power to give.

The third brother, Thomas, always more or less of an invalid, made chemical experiments, some of which led to the invention of photography. He was something of a physician, too, and given to experimenting on his elder brother's children. Eight of these, nevertheless, survived infancy, and it was again a younger son, Francis, who in 1843, became master-potter of Etruria. He was still the head of the firm when his grandson, Josiah Clement, was born at Barlaston on March 16th, 1872.

II

The village of Barlaston is a prosperous settlement some miles from Etruria, set round a triangular green on the slope of a hill not far from the infant Trent. Barlaston Hall, an eighteenth-century mansion of some pretensions, handsomely crowns the prospect, whence a pleasant stream winds down towards the river. Not far from the hall stands the church, the old tower half hidden among trees. Hither, in the middle of the nineteenth century, Francis Wedgwood, master-potter, and his family had moved their residence; every morning the working members of the family rode in from these rural uplands to the grimy hollow of the Five Towns. The prospect, on a wet Monday morning, was not always enticing for the younger members of the family, one of whom was once overheard muttering as he pulled on his boots, 'Thank God, only another forty years of this.'

On the southern side of Barlaston Green, some little distance from the hall, stood in 1872 (and still stands)

Barlaston Lea, a red-brick Staffordshire farmhouse, converted into a gentleman's residence by the addition of a handsome bow-windowed drawing-room. Before the drawing-room on the lawn flourished a cedar and a sentimental weeping ash. There were laurel shrubberies, rose beds, an ample kitchen garden and a tennis lawn. A broad ditch of water famed as an 'old moat' was later filled up for reasons of health, but a pond thickly coated with green duckweed remained. A tussocky paddock bounded by a ha-ha completed the property.

Such was the house to which Clement, the second son of the master-potter, moved shortly after his marriage to Emily Catherine Rendel. She was a serious, intelligent, well-educated young woman, the daughter of James Meadows Rendel, one of the great engineers of an age of great engineering. While hardly more than a girl she became engaged to a young man who died suddenly within a few days of the announcement. The early sorrow may have increased a certain melancholy of temperament, but she was a woman of high standards, clear judgment and the stronger virtues, and she was gravely good-looking. Clement Wedgwood, a livelier and more buoyant character, with greater gaiety and less reserve than most of his family, seems to have been drawn to her by the attraction of opposites. He was fond of hunting and of sport generally, a characteristic so rare in the family as always to cause faint amazement. His attitude to his wife was one of unstinted admiration, but the world of her London relations was strange to him and the prospect of the wedding at St. Margaret's, Westminster, caused him some apprehension. The Wedgwoods, so much at home in Staffordshire, felt embarrassed and provincial in London. Shortly before his marriage he wrote to his elder brother: 'She is the wisest and goodest person I have ever met.' The wedding proved less terrifying than he had expected and his estimate of his wife did not change with the years. Moreover, she was wholly and whole-heartedly devoted to him.

Of this happy marriage were born at two-year intervals five sons and one daughter, Frank, Harry, who died in infancy, Josiah, Ralph, Cicely and Felix. Josiah, the second son, seems to have been early his grandfather's favourite. The patriarchal old gentleman, who rose every morning to a cold saucer-bath and dumb-bell exercises in an uncarpeted room, was the presiding genius of the family in these years. Every morning, on his horse Jackdaw, he set out for the Works at so exact an hour that the villagers set their clocks by him. Age, integrity and character had made him an institution; he was not a very able man but he upheld with dignity the intellectual and radical traditions of his predecessors. He had canvassed for the Reform Bill, he had worked for the emancipation of indentured labourers and child chimney-sweeps, and he had entertained Kossuth at his house.

An established tradition governed the early education of the young Wedgwoods. As early as 1819 a visitor to the house thus described the behaviour of Josiah II and his children:

I never saw anything pleasanter than the ways of going on in this family; and one reason is the freedom of speech upon every subject. There is no difference in politics or principles of any kind that makes it treason to speak one's mind openly, and they all do it. There is a simplicity of good sense about them that no one ever dreams of not entirely differing upon any subject when they feel inclined ... The part of the intellectual character most improved by the Wedgwood education is good sense, which is indeed their pre-eminent quality. It is of the most importance and, in the end, will promote more of their own and others' happiness than any other quality. The moral quality most promoted by their education is benevolence which combined with good sense gives all that education can give . . . They have freedom in their actions in this house as in their principles. Doors and windows stand open. You are nowhere confined. You may do what you like. You are surrounded by books that all look most tempting to read. You will always find some pleasant topic of conversation or may start one, as all things are talked of in the general family.

Francis Wedgwood, himself the product of the family so described, compiled an admirable set of rules for his own children[1] and watched the growth of his grandchildren with the greatest interest. He had a deep regard for his serious-minded daughter-in-law and enjoyed the company of her children, particularly of 'your dear little Josiah', who was more delicate and more appealing than his brothers. They had their adventures and their secrets together, joined together in the hay-making and were excited and delighted on a seaside holiday when they were once cut off by the tide in each other's company.

Other yet more patriarchal presences loomed above the children, or sometimes came down to earth in smiling benevolence. Charles Darwin sometimes stayed with their grandfather, his cousin and brother-in-law. In London, there was their mother's brother, Uncle Stuart Rendel, Gladstone's friend, who organized for the little boys a tour of the underground railway with calls at each main line terminus.

---

[1] These rules are too long for quotation in the text but as a period piece they are interesting enough to put on record, and are printed in an appendix to this chapter. High principles mellowed by good nature and common sense apparently ruled this Victorian nursery.

The examples of the able, industrious, distinguished dead could be, and were, pointed out on both sides of the family. Going to the Works, the boys would pass the Trent and Mersey Canal of which 'old Josiah' had cut the first turf, and look up at his statue in the square at Stoke. A tacit reverence usually prevented the general use of the Christian name for a very young member of the family; to this day 'Siah' is the usual abbreviation for children, with promotion to 'Jos' in later life. At Portland, little Siah was shown the docks his other grandfather had built. He and his brothers grew up naturally into a tradition of achievement and endeavour and public duties.

Such were the more distant benevolent presences in the youth of Josiah and his brothers. Their father was a close and constant one. He had a natural gift for the pleasures of childhood. He took them on a trip down a coal-mine, and all over the engine works at Stratford and Crewe. He built them toy railways and on their holidays on the Northumbrian coast initiated them into the joys of exploration and map-making. He hung head-downward over rock pools searching for weird anemones and curious fish, and shortened the longest walk for their short legs with the unfailing invention of stories. After tea at Barlaston on winter evenings he read aloud while the boys, with paper outspread to protect the tablecloth, painted maps of imaginary regions.

Some of their children's books have been handed down, delightful French books with steel engravings on every page, *Les Commandements de Grandpapa*, *l'Histoire de Monsieur Vieux Bois* and *The Story of a Round Loaf*. But in the evenings their father did not read children's books to them, and, as they daubed happily away, the solid classics of English liberalism poured into their — intermittently attentive — ears: Macaulay, Motley, Kinglake, Froude. Not by any means did all of it remain, but in their minds certain phrases and certain ideas insensibly collected: a sediment of principles — prejudices, if you will: admiration for courage, respect for honesty, hatred of injustice and oppression, the belief that right is more than might and the conviction that right will triumph.

Such principles, strongly held, characterized their mother too. She was a woman of upright and distinguished character with a high respect for learning. Italian and French she knew well, German sufficiently; although she was not quite at home with classical Greek she loved to read the Greek Testament aloud with her sons, a custom which she continued until late in life with her eldest son Frank. The feat of knowledge which was later to be held up for her grandchildren to marvel at was less attractive but illustrates well the Victorian insistence on the hard grit of facts; she knew the name and capital of every Department in France.

In his *Memoirs of a Fighting Life* Josiah gratefully described her translating Homer to him as she went along. This was an endearing exaggeration; all his life he had the charming quality of investing those he loved with the abilities they themselves would most have liked to possess. Yet, whether she read the *Iliad* to her children in her own translation or that of Dr. Church (with the Flaxman illustrations of course, since Flaxman had designed for Wedgwood) — the upshot was the same. She peopled Barlaston for her children with the mighty names of antiquity.

Siah was not as strong as his brothers, hence, perhaps, a lack of assurance which found expression in a more winning courtship of approbation than was usual in this self-sufficient, robustly self-confident family. His childhood, for that reason, was probably not quite so happy as that of his brothers; but the picture which my father, his next brother, Ralph, has given of it suggests that it was happy nevertheless:

When we were children we often used to argue, between joke and earnest, which of us was the favourite son. My mother would say, half-embarrassed, that she had no favourite — or that her favourite was always the one who wanted her most at the moment — but that didn't pass, and the vote fell generally upon Jos. I hadn't really much opinion on the matter, but I can see now that it was true, and why it was so.

We were self-sufficient; he needed, and sought for, outside approval. My mother felt his loneliness, and answered his unspoken call for support; in return, he gave her what no other child of hers, at that time, could give — the personal sympathy and the words of praise that warmed her heart. That social gift remained with him through life.

Looking back on it, I feel that he was always rather 'odd man out' at home. His happiest days, I suspect, were those which he and I shared in the schoolroom under the care of the voluble, adventurous young woman who was our governess. She led us on to try sweeping the chimney on our own — I can still see Jos robed in a white sheet (I can't think why) with a chimney-brush in his hand; they went through with it, but I hung back, afraid.

At home, when my father came back from work, he used to give us history lessons — almost daily, it seems, as I look back, and the history he taught us had nothing parochial about it. It covered the whole world. Its text-book was *Bicknell's Dates* which traced the history of all the races of the world, in parallel columns, from the creation; and by a bold inaccuracy fixed the dates of the great events in a boy's mind for ever. My father's period was the Roman Empire, and as we sat upon his knee, or leant upon his chair, Jos and I would call out in turn — 'One-one-one Trajan', 'Two-two-

two Alexander Severus', 'Three-three-three Constantine', 'Four-four-four Sack of Rome' — so it went on until history lost its romance at the point where most children begin to read it. Frank was always the leader: he started nearly all our tastes — soldiers, maps, railways — but we developed them in our own way.

With us, mythology was the first stage and militarism the second. One of my earliest memories is of marching round and round the nursery table — I can see its surface, level with my eye, even now — number three to Frank and Jos as one and two while we all sang in never-ending chorus 'Hercules, Theseus, and wary-wise Odysseus' — to be wary-wise was not heroic, but as the third son I could only expect the lowest place in the series.

Soon the *Lays of Ancient Rome* swept the board — *Lake Regillus* first, with *Horatius* close behind, and the rest nowhere. I can't tell from what early date we all knew those two poems by heart — repeated them to our elders, acted them and parodied them, but never tired of them. To the end of his life, you could start Jos on them anywhere and he could complete the verse.

Then there was the lead-soldier epoch. Frank began it, and it was always one of his lamentations that we younger brothers had taken possession of his great army and broken the soldiers. It may have been true: those old lead soldiers were easily broken, but how good they were. It is another lost art, and though it was a German one it is still worthy of its special record and regret. The ideal lead soldiers must not be too large — one inch, at most, in height, and they must all be of one standard height. They must not be too realistic — movable arms and legs are for children, or for grown-ups who don't understand, a signpost on the road to decay. The true art reached its height with those oblong cardboard boxes, shaped like a brick, white with blue scroll work, and blue German print of which I only remember the words 'Fein, Massiv'. For long enough they were the unit of coinage to Jos and to me — they cost a shilling each in the Arcade at Bournemouth. If there was something else to be bought for a shilling, the question with us was always — 'Is it worth a box of soldiers?' and the answer, generally, 'No.' From these boxes, there poured out regiment after regiment of Prussian soldiers, in dark blue, of Bavarians in light blue, Russians in green — some French too, and a few English in red, or the black of the Rifle Brigade. Cavalry, too, with dismountable horsemen (the only recognized concession to realism), and guns, which ran on wheels, and were all the better if they could fire small peas. I could weep still to think how the art has fallen — like so many others by the pursuit of naturalism, and the neglect of the inner symbolism. No boy, not even a millionaire's son, could build up a proper army in these degenerate days. Our armies ran into thousands and great battles were fought over the schoolroom floor — the greatest of all perhaps was fought one Easter holidays when some boy's sickness prevented Jos from going back to school, and canvas screens were spread across his bed, loaded with real earth for hedges and entrenchments. We fought no 'replica' battles, nor did any real military hero set us a model for imitation, but there was some science nevertheless about our campaigns, and we owed that to my father. He had been a keen militia officer, and had practised the 'War Game'. From his cupboards he unearthed a set of 6-inch ordnance maps (of the Aldershot area), pasted on drawing-boards: a wooden box, too, full of little lead pieces, each representing a battalion, a squadron, a battery, vedette, units in column of march, in line of battle, or in open order; and, with these, elaborate tables for calculating (with the aid of the dice box) speed of march, effectiveness of fire (direct or enfilade) and a dozen other particularities. Most of all, he taught us to work out from the configuration of the map, what each commander could see, or not see, of the other's movements. It was a great game, when he could preside over it, but by ourselves we reverted to our lead soldiers, merely using his tables (and the dice), to calculate the casualties in the charging columns. Then it all faded out as Jos grew up, and by the time he was sixteen our army was no more. Felix's soldiers were never more than toys.

Whether maps or railways came first I do not know. We three elder boys were always neat with our figures, and we could always occupy a rainy day by drawing maps of imaginary countries. Jos drew a whole Continent and set out to write the history of it. My father joined in once — on his way to some evening appointment: he contributed the statement that Fenlac, King of Vensulala, invented the leg of mutton, and followed this up with an account of the contest between the Blues and the Greens, when faction demanded that even the leaves of the trees should be painted blue — a reminiscence of Gibbon and the factions of the Circus. The History died out in echoes of Justin MacCarthy's *History of Our Own Times*. The rhetorical Irish style found its way at every turn into the imaginary histories we wrote — the exiled king found a subsistence 'as a fisherman on the icy banks of the Otenfrod', or sought sword in hand to restore his kingdom 'until a grey-goose-shaft cut short his chequered career'. Such flowers of eloquence have always had their appeal for Jos; but Justin MacCarthy did more. With his admirations and enthusiasms he kindled Jos's political imagination, and the glow remained, always ready to blaze up, however other interests might overlay it.

Every summer we travelled north to a 'shooting' in Northumberland, or (later) Scotland. It was the great event in our lives, and to the last Jos could have given you the date and the place for each migration. Within a few weeks of his death, I reminded him of how we two used to escape into the kitchen-garden at Lesbury, crawl in among the Jerusalem artichokes, and hew them down with a table-knife, pretending that we were away in the backwoods, and how we hid from the gardeners. 'That must have been in 1880,' I said. 'No, '81' he replied, with perfect certainty.

That was real travelling. The whole family migrated, complete with servants. The saloon stood in the siding at Barlaston, and we all packed in before the train arrived — later, when we went to Scotland, it became a saloon-sleeping-car: we travelled up over-night, and the first daylight found us far away. (That was how I first saw the Shap Fells, lying

in an upper berth with my eyes glued to three inches of
window, as the grey fells rolled and clanked past me to the
rolling and clanking of the train, and the engine toiled up
the last ascent. They had an unearthly goblin-like look in
the misty dawn; and for me they have never lost that feeling.)
But the journey to Northumberland was full of excitement —
the saloon was transferred at Stockport and Stalybridge —
they were names of romance to us, and well they might be —
'This is the stone-wall country!' my father shouted between
our craning heads, against the rattling of the train — and I
can see now the little grey town clustered round its church,
and the ragged stone walls that stretched up to the sky-line.
My mother was kept busy getting the cinders out of our
eyes, for we never left the open window. 'Here's a bridge
coming!' and down it went in our book. A station flew past
— with caps crammed on we watched for the name — 'Mars-
den' one of us shouted. There was a hiss of steam — an
engine standing in the Bay Platform 'Thirteen-Twenty-
Seven', with a cry of triumph, 'but I couldn't read its name,
because of the steam!' 'Never mind the names — they're
frauds' said Frank, remembering how in two successive years
we had found the same name on two different engines.

One year we had 'the Directors' saloon' with a wide
window looking forward. We plunged into the Standedge
Tunnel, and against the rolling smoke from the engine (we
were the first carriage on the train) we could see the fireman
lit by the glare from the fire-box as he shovelled the coal
forward. At the first stop after the tunnel he came back to
talk to us — we besieged him with questions. He wiped his
hands and enjoyed the game, and rolled out the names of
the stations we had passed.

At the end of the journey we went through the numbers,
crossing out those that were 'stale'. Frank entered the new
numbers in the book, each in the colour appropriate to its
company. The book, with the numbers entered in his clear
precise hand, is still extant — he kept it up to the last (until
he left Cambridge, in fact), with periodical censuses and
'bumping-sheets'.

If Frank was, and remained, our leader in 'catching numbers' Jos led the way in Bradshaw. He was a great map-drawer, and soon a map was incomplete without its railways — more, the railways must have their Bradshaw. Jos was the first of us, indeed the only one of us, to draw up a complete 'Bradshaw' covering every railway in his imaginary country with all their cross-connections. But the imaginary always gave way to the real. There was a time when every holiday, Jos and I set out to paint a Bradshaw Map — no easy task. We extracted the paper map from a Bradshaw, we got a paint-box and 'etching' pens: then while one of us read each entry from the Bradshaw summary the other traced the lines on the map in the colour appropriate to each company. It was a triumph when the map was finished, though to the last there were some lines still un-coloured — lines shown on the map but not mentioned in the summary, or even in the body of Bradshaw (Fenny-Stratford—Towcester—Stratford-on-Avon was one). Even grown-ups shook their heads and owned themselves defeated.

An outer circle of cousins surrounded this inner circle of brothers. There were something like fifty of them. The younger ones, I learn from one of them, regarded Siah as their favourite. His own concealed shyness and need for help made him sympathetic to the smaller children whom he never patronized and whom he liked to guide on expeditions of chivalry and daring. It was a characteristic which persisted throughout life.

III

As a child and in later life Josiah undoubtedly found family surroundings sustaining. The family was something that he needed although it was not for many years that his love took the form of a deep interest in family history. But the intense feeling which was to make him tell his daughter Camilla, much later in life, that 'no friend in the world can mean as much to me as brothers and sisters' grew up in those early days.

Looking back after sixty years he still resented the decree which packed him off to school 'among thirty-five other small savages' at the age of ten. A preparatory school can grow so appalling in the memory of a pupil who was unhappy at it that it is impossible to guess what it was really like. The end-of-term hymn, which ran:

> Home, safe home, at last,
> Rent cordage, tattered sail

seems fitly to have expressed Josiah's feeling about the whole miserable business.

He did not distinguish himself at his preparatory school, but he did better at Clifton whither in 1885 he followed his eldest brother. Frank was already a popular figure in the house and known to all the school. With this good start, Josiah quickly found his feet. Before he left, he had found confidence and made himself a circle of friends some of whom remained with him all his life. When he reached the sixth he had no difficulty in exercising authority. It came to him naturally without the need for assertion.

By the time Ralph got to Clifton, Josiah had already gone over to the Military and Engineering side. Modern subjects suited his taste better than the Classics for which he had never much use except as a source of sonorous quotations. He joined the School Rifle Corps as soon as he got there, and later made his more intellectual younger brother, Ralph, join it too. 'On half-holidays,' my father remembers, 'we would toil down together (carrying our rifles), through Bristol to the Bedminster Rifle Range, and fire off our seven rounds, first at the two hundred, and then at the five hundred yard targets, with Dundry steeple looking down upon us from the middle distance. Then a cup of tea, with "Garibaldi" biscuits ("squashed flies" we called them), and home to Clifton. To me it was a dreary degrading business, but then I seldom hit the target. Jos ended by shooting for the School.'

It was in the School Debating Society that he began first to develop his interest in politics, and at once evinced a taste for minorities. 'Last night,' he wrote to his mother, 'we had a debate whether Home Rule ought to be had or not; I was one of the five who voted for it. I voted for it because so few did.' His leading characteristic was established thus early. A little later the cause of Liberalism, not then popular among schoolboys, began to look up. In a debate on the abolition of the House of Lords — 'for once the Liberals won,' reported Jos. 'The house was abolished by a preponderance of six.'

'Aren't the elections terribly exciting?' he wrote home in November 1885 when Gladstone and Salisbury were contesting under the shadow of the Gordon episode. The struggle was reflected in the debating society. 'I spoke for the opposition which won. My speech was a great success, especially a little I put in about the Conservatives.' His prowess in speaking improved with practice; a year later in another Home Rule debate, he carried enough of the house with him to win, by a single vote.

Occasionally visiting parents joined in the debate and my father has recorded one such occasion:

One Michaelmas Term my father and mother came down to Clifton — our debate that week was on education and Jos led the House for Free Education. How the debate ended I don't remember, but my father was invited to speak and took part. He spoke modestly, drawing from his experience on the Hanley School Board (he was Chairman), and coming down strongly in favour of compulsory education. 'On the question of payment,' he said, 'there is much more room for doubt. I don't think I am called upon to express an opinion one way or the other, but I think there is weight in the argument that people are apt to set little value on what they get for nothing.' We both felt proud of him — there was never a parent less like Mr. Bultitude.

Not long afterwards this best of fathers fell ill and Josiah's last term at school was clouded with anxiety, although he had the pleasure of reporting one triumph — his winning of the Gold Medal for history. This gave real joy to his father, who had his son's papers, composed in the style of Gibbon, read aloud to him in his sick-room. He died a few weeks later. During the months that followed, Josiah was his mother's constant companion and found both comfort and just pride in realizing how much his support meant to her. She grieved deeply for a loss which was to her truly irreparable, but her well-disciplined mind did not permit her to waste the hours, either for herself or her son. It was during the months immediately following his father's death, while Frank was at Cambridge and Ralph still at school, that she and Josiah undertook the strenuous course of reading in modern languages to which he owed his fluency in French and his knowledge of Dante.

He had always been attracted towards the Army, but the year of his father's death brought another disappointment, for, although he passed into Woolwich, he failed to get through the medical tests. Pending further decisions on his career, it was decided to send him to Germany. In Dresden he had an aunt, his father's sister Rose, with a German husband and two German nieces. It was decided that he should pass some months with them to learn the language and continue his general education. His diary of the period survives, a conscientious, not very illuminating document, which, after a surprisingly short lapse of time, breaks from English into fluent, incorrect, comprehensible German: evidently a nightly exercise self-imposed.

At first he missed the atmosphere and the landscape of England. 'In this benighted country,' he wrote home, 'they have no hedges, flowers or lanes and precious few trees. As for the people they excell [sic] in taking off their hats and in nothing else.' He himself certainly did not excel in spelling. Unmusical, he sat in gloom through four and a half hours of Wagner, which were not cheered by the intervals in which he found himself compelled to make conversation to a 'fashionably languid' English girl.

Soon, however, he found his feet, became more responsive to the countryside, and, as his vocabulary increased, more understanding of the German character and its virtues. He grew into a vigorous rather than a correct linguist; comprehensibility and fluency were what he sought to acquire, rather than a slavish exactitude. In after years he would surprise — and usually charm — German-speaking audiences by telling them at the outset that he intended to use the article 'der' for all cases and genders.

The sentimental young ladies in Dresden soon indulged in the *schwärmerei* natural to their age. He does not seem always fully to have understood their manœuvres, although he listened sympathetically when they made him share their sensibilities and sorrows, but when one of them opened up with the old gambit: 'Why are you so indifferent to me? You

English are so cold . . .' he seems to have been
thoroughly puzzled. Or else he was not being frank
to his diary.

After three months of Dresden he was evidently
bored, and in the winter he moved to a more entertaining family in Weimar. Here the daughters of the
house wrote novels and studied their paying guests
for copy. They also indulged in parties, some of them
in fancy dress; Josiah gratified his romantic temperament by appearing as a character from Schiller's
Don Carlos, though whether as the libertarian Marquis
Posa or the hapless prince himself it is impossible to
tell from the surviving photograph. He was of course
cramming his receptive memory with stirring phrases
from Goethe and Schiller for future quotation. Typically, however, his favourite German tag in after life
had strong military associations. 'Ich kenne meine
Pappenheimer,' he would approvingly quote from
Wallenstein as his children charged out of a shrubbery,
or at other moments of recognition.

Before his time was up at Weimar he had assisted at
his first election and seen the *Freisinnige Volkspartei*
win amid scenes of sober enthusiasm. He admired
German liberalism, German social progress and German education. But he was contemptuous of the
conventions of German society and of the general
subservience towards authority.

Meanwhile, his mother's brother, Hamilton Rendel,
a partner in Armstrong's, the great ship-builders, who
now stood in lieu of father to the boys, had offered to
send him to Cambridge, but he refused. He wanted
something more active and it was decided that he
should join his uncle in Newcastle and learn to be a
naval architect.

His mother felt, however, that one more season

should be allowed to culture. Another of her brothers, George Rendel who controlled Armstrong's Italian factory at Pozzuoli, lived near Naples at Posilippo; in the spring of 1890 she brought out her daughter Cicely on a visit, combining the family reunion with an instructive tour of the sights in which Josiah was included. From the terrace of his uncle's villa he heard the Neopolitan boatmen singing 'Funicolí, funicolá' and 'Santa Lucia', the only tunes (with the exception of the Land Song and the Hatikvah) that ever fixed themselves in his unmusical mind.

After Naples, they toured the Italian cities, assisted by Baedeker, Ruskin and Sismondi. Josiah's Italian was never as good as his German, but it could be effective. At Pisa a touting guide climbed on to the box of their cab and would not be driven away. Josiah rose to his feet, extended his open palm before the man's face, then striking it with his pointed fore-finger, exclaimed: 'Io so Pisa come la mano: vià.' The resonance rather than the words made the meaning clear and the man fled. The phrase, in the manner of such trifles, still survives as a family saying.

He enjoyed Italy, but his attitude to the arts was one rather of dutiful than of spontaneous admiration. He had left Dresden convinced that the Sistine Madonna was the Most Beautiful Picture in the World; he used it, with an endearing simplicity, as his yard-stick for measuring aesthetic values to the end of his life, and when in the wreck of a Boer farmstead fifteen years later he found a framed photograph of it under a badly cracked glass he carefully salvaged it. It was a token of his respect for Art.

But he had not the aesthetic temperament and he was already longing for a life of constructive work and

strenuous leisure. He left Italy therefore with no regret, and proceeded to Newcastle where, in September
1890, he unpacked his trunks in Uncle Hamilton's
spare room, and set off with unaffected eagerness to
his first day's real work.

APPENDIX TO CHAPTER I

RULES FOR THE NURSERY COMPILED ABOUT 1840 BY FRANCIS
WEDGWOOD, MASTER-POTTER OF ETRURIA, GRANDFATHER OF
JOSIAH CLEMENT WEDGWOOD

The strictest habits of truth being of first rate importance
they should be carefully cultivated in every way.

No question should be asked which would give a temptation to lie, such as inquiring who broke the cup? or spilt the
ink? or cut a hole in the table cloth? or so on. If you do not
know who did it you must be content to shew disapprobation
without fixing on the particular culprit. Mere careless-
ness I should never think of punishing, but I had rather
any amount of wanton mischief went undetected than
throw the least temptation to lie in the way of any of the
children.

Every lie — besides its own particular evil — has the
additional disadvantage that it makes the next easier to
conscience.

It is a great matter never to shew suspicion of a child —
even when you do suspect deceit, you should take care not
to show it. Take all the pains you can to get to the bottom
of it, and when you are quite sure of the deceit, never pass it
over without making your disapprobation strongly felt. Any
little cunning tricks, such as children have to get some little
advantage I always think are best unnoticed, but at the same
time I take care to thwart them. Cunning should never

succeed — neither should it be treated as a sin because it is not one. In general I think regular preachments to little children do no good but harm and great care is necessary not to make too much of a fault and tell a child it is 'very wicked' for every trifle. Most children may be made to feel that they are wrong almost without scolding at all — from the manner merely of those they love. A fault confessed should never be punished at all. The shame of the confession is punishment enough, and openness and candour are qualities to be encouraged by every possible expedient. Of course if the confession was a mere impudent expedient to escape punishment — it would be a different thing — but I have no fear of that.

The article of tale-telling is rather difficult to manage; on one hand they should never be taught to conceal anything from their parents or governess, on the other hand they ought to feel a dislike to bring brother or sister into disgrace. The only way I know is to judge of the motive as well as you can by the manner, and act accordingly. If the motive is (as I am afraid it generally is), 'See how much better I am' a little mortifying coldness will be well applied. If the motive is spite I should take care that the scolding should light on the tale-bearer's shoulders — instead of the other's — but then, if possible, it should be made plain that it is the feeling you reprobate and not the simple act of telling. Shame and ridicule are two instruments that are sometimes used to children, which in my opinion are utterly and entirely inadmissible. Ridicule they feel in an acute way that grownup folk have no conception of — and they get to hate people that use it towards them. Shame is not the proper feeling to excite for a fault — sorrow is. With young children jokes should be avoided — they never understand them but they see it is meant for a joke and they receive it with an affected laugh and so they lose what is their peculiar charm, simplicity.

On the subject of truth — Precision of expression is to be cultivated and all hyperbolical expressions avoided, such as 'a hundred times' when you mean perhaps twenty — 'twice as big' when the thing is not really near twice as big. It is very difficult to make children understand these are not 'lies'; for the same reason when a child corrects any expression of that sort — as for instance if you say 'Half a dozen' and the child says 'No, it was seven' — the correction should be received with encouragement.

Promises are always to be kept with the greatest strictness — both by the children and towards them — and therefore great caution should be used in making them promises and even in saying what you are going to do — for the nature of a promise is not very clear in their minds. I have several times been puzzled to explain why when I said I was going to do so and so it was not a promise to do it which bound me — and have been obliged to do it (though no promise), because it seemed one to them. Promises should never be taken from them — it is a great trap for veracity. If they promise one another — they must perform.

The next virtue in a child after truth is obedience. The great matter is never to order but what is reasonable — and when you do order always to insist on obedience and at once if possible. In the same way as traps for truth are to be avoided — so are traps for obedience. Thus you must not give them general orders to do so and so every day and expect to be obeyed — it is not in the nature of children to do it. A general order never to do so and so does not stand in the same predicament. Many such orders are necessary and they are obeyed. The difference is that the breach of the command not to do so and so is a precise act, which they feel when they are doing — but the breach of the general order to do so and so at such and such a time, is not a precise act, they never feel that they are disobeying as long as they are going to do it, and so they go dawdling on until the time is past, and so get habits of dawdling and disobedience at once. It is a lazy way of managing children to tell them what they have to do once, and then expect it to be done regularly, and then scold if it is not — this will never succeed — the only way with children is to tell them when the times come 'Now go and do so and so' — and to see that they do

37

it — and this over and over again, till they have got into a habit of it.

Patience and Perseverance are the two great requisites for a teacher. No trouble should be thought too great to break habits of dawdling — of all habits not absolutely wrong it is the worst. I tried rewards, when I had the management of children, for though I would never reward good conduct properly so called (which would be giving children wrong motives), yet I think rewards for exertions stand on a different footing. All through life exertions not only meet with rewards — but it is the rewards that they meet with that stimulate them.

Giving a child a task to do of itself without overlooking it is bad — because it is sure to get into a dilatory, dawdling way of doing it. Thus in arithmetic I object to the common way of setting a sum and 'Come to me when you have done it' — the child goes into a corner and learns a very little arithmetic and a great deal of dawdling — and the longer he is about his sum the more he hates it. All sums should be done aloud at the teacher's elbow and no dawdling allowed. This is the great merit of questions to be done by the head without a slate at all.

Habits of order and tidiness are of great value; the way to get them is not to tell children once what they have to do and then make a fault of it whenever they do not do it; but by seeing that they do everything of that kind when it is to be done and in the right way.

Emulation which is a very useful help in teaching a school is inadmissible amongst brothers and sisters — far from wishing them to take pains to outstrip one another, I should be delighted to see each of them better pleased with a brother's or sister's success than its own.

Much may be done by judicious management in fostering affectionate giving up to one another. For instance, my girl comes complaining 'Papa, brother won't lend me his pencil'. My first care is to put a right feeling into the girl's mind and I say: 'Oh, I am sure he will if you ask him good-humouredly ... try.' Generally this is enough — but if not I next take

38

the boy in hand and tell him how much nicer it is of brothers and sisters to be good-natured to one another — still taking care that all the merit of yielding should belong to him and all the gratitude (if any) should be felt towards him. If the boy still is obdurate I content myself by showing that I am not pleased. If it was a case of injustice, as if the pencil was the girl's, I should proceed in the same way (only if gentle means failed I should insist on justice being done), because if one asks as a favour what the other gives as a favour, there is a kindly feeling on both sides; but if the matter is claimed as a right and given up as it were by force there is likely to be some feeling of bitterness; but even this must be risked rather than give up the paramount principle that no injustice must be allowed amongst them. Under the head of mutual kindness, snappish hasty tones and answers may be mentioned. They should always be checked at the time. Any little unkind action I think it is best to reprove the next time you have the delinquent alone. On the other hand kindnesses should be encouraged in every way.

Children's eternal questions are very often troublesome enough and people are apt to check them either by dry cold answers or telling them to hold their tongues — now inasmuch as a child will learn twice as much of anything he is interested in, I look upon it that the answering questions readily and in a way rather to encourage than discourage them — is one very material branch of education. In particular, no question should be answered in a bantering way; children as I said before cannot abide it. What one has to do is to give them all the information one can — in an agreeable shape and in a way that they will understand.

Children are so apt to be made vain and affected, and are so open to any sort of flattery — that I have always found it a good rule never to repeat any of their sayings or doings — either before the one who said or did — or even before any of the others.

Telling of dreams — I have always discouraged — as I think it leads to lying. No books are allowed as playthings.

39

If pictures are looked at, the book must be laid on something and not on the child's knees, for the sake of the books. No books to be carried out-of-doors, nor out of the room at all without leave. It is a great help in the management of children to go by rules: they always submit to a rule, I find, without any feeling of hardship. With regard to the length of their lessons — I would rather they were underdone than overdone. I think the boy of about nine might manage three or four hours a day — and the girls of about six and seven two hours a day, each including everything. I wish them to go out twice a day unless it rains, but to come in again as soon as they like. I should like them to be out whenever they are not at their lesson in summer if they would.

CHAPTER II

AN EARNEST YOUNG MAN

'I HAVE become one of the aristocrats of Labour,'
wrote Josiah to his younger brother Ralph in
February 1891, some months after he had started
work in the Elswick shipyard. Fifty years later he
still remembered the enthusiasm and the absorbed
pleasure with which he had learnt the craft of 'that
closest and richest of Trade Unions, the Boiler-
makers and Shipwrights'. After the unrewarding
struggle of his school years he had found the job which
fascinated him and gave him confidence. He was on
top of the world. 'Six foot high with a cloth cap,
scarf tied round the neck, white moleskin trousers,
with a hammer poking out of one pocket and a steel
rule out of another, I swaggered down to work with a
sense of mastery that no office job can ever supply.'

Both his political and literary education progressed.
During the day he talked politics with his fellow-
workers and got on with them very well, although he
once annoyed the foreman by reading Alfieri's
Congiura dei Pazzi while he cut cog-wheels — processes
which he asserted could easily be combined. In the
evenings, seated in an easy chair by the comfortable
fireside of Uncle Hamilton's Victorian house he read
Napoleonic memoirs, the better known English
novels, and Napier's *Peninsular War*, some of which he
carefully learnt by heart. The grandeurs of the
military profession still appealed to him; they did so
to the end of his life. 'A man I envy is Marbot,' he
wrote to Ralph. 'He charges every day at the head of
his squadrons and is wounded twice a year on an

average.' He also wished to borrow from home for his bedroom in Newcastle the handsome steel engraving of Delaroche's 'Napoleon at St. Helena'.

In the midst of his further education in history and literature he stumbled on Edward Bellamy's *Looking Backward*. Published in America in 1888 this fantasy of the future had swept gradually forward to international fame. The Utopia, which Bellamy depicted in the year 2000, was founded on the abolition of capital and the comprehensive organization of education and labour. It owes something to other and earlier Utopias and its political and economic structure will not bear close examination, but it contains some impassioned writing on the conditions of the submerged poor in the contemporary world:

From the black doorways and windows of the rookeries on every side came gusts of fetid air. The streets and alleys reeked with the effluvia of a slave ship's between-decks. As I passed I had glimpses within of pale babies gasping out their lives amid sultry stenches, of hopeless-faced women deformed by hardship . . . while from the windows leered girls with brows of brass . . . Swarms of half-clad brutalized children filled the air with shrieks and curses as they fought and tumbled among the garbage that littered the courtyards . . . Presently, too, as I observed the wretched beings about me more closely, I perceived that they were all quite dead. Their bodies were so many living sepulchres. On each brutal brow was plainly written the *hic jacet* of a soul dead within.

Such passages, combined with the Utopian conditions which Bellamy depicted as the result of his economic panacea, deeply moved the young Josiah as indeed they have many another sensitive, intelligent and conscientious young man and woman. It is, however, worth emphasizing, at this early stage of his political awakening, that he saw injustice and oppression as the enemies, and the freedom and dignity of each individual human being as the goal, nor did he ever believe, as Bellamy undoubtedly did, in the total direction of society by even the most benevolent of States. Later in life he declared that Bellamy had made him a Socialist, but he was always — often to the embarrassment of his colleagues — a Socialist of a highly unorthodox kind.

Meanwhile, a little to Uncle Hamilton's dismay, he threw himself into the new cause, saw much of James Clare, an official in the Miners' Union and subsequently Councillor and Alderman of Newcastle, and when Ralph came up to visit him, took him off at once, in Clare's company, to address a meeting on Old Age Pensions in a mining village. This must have been one of Josiah's earliest political speeches and he was not so much at home with his mining audience as he had been in the School Debating Society. 'Jos's speech,' as my father recollected it, 'was what you would expect from a very young man, rather afraid of his audience — alternately timid and over-bold, with jokes and epigrams they did not understand. He had no natural flow of words, and no natural magnetism for an audience. It was by sheer persistence, and the determination not to be beaten, that he made himself the speaker he afterwards became.' His struggles, like those of Demosthenes, were long and weary; he has recorded some of them in his autobiography.

James Clare also took him to the Trades Union Congress of 1891, where he met John Burns and other pioneer Socialists and was exhilarated and impressed. Many political winds blew through his brain, international or libertarian. The death of the staunch rationalist Bradlaugh moved him to epigrammatic regret in a letter to Ralph: 'He was one of the few men who have some backbone and who stick to their principles, not principals.' Like most keen young men he was appalled at the spinelessness and acquiescence of his elders in so much that was wrong, so much that he and his friends could soon put right. A few days later he heard a Russian nihilist address a meeting on his experiences while in prison in Siberia and glowed with avenging anger against the Tsar. With a little encouragement how gladly would he have set out on a mission of tyranicide, stepping, like Browning's mysterious Waring,

> Over the Kremlin's pavement, bright
> With serpentine and syenite ...

to make an end of the despot.

In October came the climax of the political year for the Liberals of Newcastle, with the visit of Mr. Gladstone. 'He is a very tottering old man,' wrote Josiah, 'but he made no bones about making himself heard over the theatre for one and a half hours.' Later, he was privately brought in to the presence by his cousin Maud, Henry Gladstone's wife. The interview was disappointing to the ardent young radical of nineteen: Mr. Gladstone spoke at length of old Josiah and the beauty of his ware, and young Josiah — as he afterwards complained to Ralph — could not get a word in edgeways.

The account he gave half a century later in his autobiography is a little different. He got in a whole sentence. 'Mr. Gladstone, sir,' he said, 'nous sommes nous même des ancêtres.' The patriarch's answer rumbled like thunder among the hills. 'Young man, I hope you will live long enough to realize the value of good traditions.'

Between the two accounts, the second may well be

the more correct. Josiah at nineteen almost certainly had the confidence to address these words to Gladstone just as, at nineteen, he found it embarrassing to record the snub when describing the interview. But the words sank in and, by his own account, first directed his attention to the study of genealogy which in after years was to occupy much of his leisure.

He had not been long at Elswick before he tried out his skill in ship-building. His first personal achievement in his profession of naval architect was a canoe, called the *Santa Lucia* after his favourite song. The little craft was truly built; she has outlasted her youthful architect and carries his descendants today over the tranquil water of the Trent and Mersey canal.

After a year at Newcastle Josiah, now fully absorbed in his chosen profession of naval architect, went up to London to work for a scholarship to the Royal Naval College at Greenwich. He lived with another uncle, Meadows Rendel, whose three handsome daughters, but more especially the eldest, Edith, taught him the ways of society.

His first love in London seems to have been this friendly, sociable cousin who took him calling and taught him the polite opening phrases for social small talk. But some time before he moved south he had made the acquaintance of another of his London cousins who was gradually to absorb him altogether. This was Ethel Bowen, daughter of his mother's sister and Lord Bowen the then famous witty judge.

Ethel, who lived with her family in Prince Albert Gate, was a handsome, intelligent, extremely serious woman, a year or two older than her cousin. All the autumn and winter of 1892 she and Josiah were going about together, sometimes a little to the dismay of her family whom she treated with unvictorian

ruthlessness. The two young people took themselves
and their ideas with great solemnity. A difference of
opinion on the merits of a Rossetti caused a serious
tiff in the National Gallery. But there were subjects
on which they agreed; they demolished Herbert
Spencer to their common satisfaction, and about the
Fabian movement their pulses beat as one. He had
become a Fabian as soon as he reached Woolwich,
taking an early opportunity of calling on Edward
Pease at the Fabian Society office in order to learn all
he could about the cause. He told Ethel of the first
lecture he attended, how he sat on a hard bench and
listened to an interminable list of statistics in broken
English from the lecturer — but, he concluded, bright-
ening, there were splendid questions from the working
men in the audience. 'I am getting up the subject of
municipalizing bakehouses and providing breakfasts
at board-schools.' Such were the sentiments with
which he concluded a letter to his beloved.

Her responses were in much the same tone, dealing
with Mr. Gladstone and the Aliens Bill, and a speech
by the working-man M.P. for Middlesborough. On
one occasion when her mother was ill, she was called
upon to take the opposite end of her father's dinner-
table when Gladstone and the Archbishop of Canterbury were the guests. Jos encouraged her — a little
enviously, perhaps; he would have liked to be present
himself, but was not. Too young, too raw, too radical?
In any case it went off well and in the relief she
scribbled to him suggesting that next time they met
they should 'do something a little vagabondish'.
Eluding chaperones, they walked daringly in Kensing-
ton Gardens, even in Richmond Park until Lord
Bowen — knowing that his daughter would always do
as she wished — sent for the young cousin and put him

on his honour to avoid such unconventional conduct.

Meanwhile he had won his scholarship, and before entering the Royal Naval College joined his two brothers for a canoeing tour in Germany. They went down the Danube from Donaueschingen to Ulm, crossed over to the Jagst, but on finding it too shallow for navigation crossed to the Neckar at Heilbronn and proceeded to the junction of the Rhine and so, northwards, to Cologne, camping among vineyards and romantic scenery while Josiah did most of the cooking. It was the last holiday the three brothers spent together and it ended in the unforgettable splendour of a slap-up dinner at the Hotel du Nord at Cologne, where a wealthy uncle and aunt made the campers welcome to a civilized meal accompanied by sparkling hock — nectar to their palates.

Back in London, and at work at Greenwich, Josiah saw much of Ethel Bowen. Slowly their conversation graduated from the condition of the working classes to the condition of their hearts. In April 1893 she wrote declaring that they must part for ever and followed it up with a wire demanding his instant presence. By May of course they were engaged. Ethel approached the matter with high socialist principles: 'One thing remember, I will never have anything to do with a rich man, a creature who has four-course dinners and is waited on by servants. You are a working man and I am a working woman . . . Don't let's be like the characters in Besant's novels who always start on purely Socialist principles with a cheque for £100,000 in their pockets and the succession to an earldom . . . Get me made a Fabianess. If you know any Fabian work that I could do I shall be very glad of it . . . our life together ought to be splendid.'

The two families were agreed that Josiah at barely

twenty was too young. (Ethel was three years older.) He was still in the first year of his course at Greenwich; they must wait until the end of his third year. At first they appeared willing. They met at week-ends and during the interminable weeks were prolific of correspondence. She threw herself with passion not only into politics but into mathematics, making drawings of transverse stresses which he showed with pride to fellow-students. Often he was able to gladden her with their comments: 'I say, Wedgwood,' they exclaimed, 'your young woman is a brick.'

Writing to each other was, for the greater part of the time, their only outlet. He from his lodgings in Dulwich, she from the lofty bedroom in Prince Albert Gate poured forth their awkward, youthful handwriting. Lovelace, he used to say later with pride, could have done no better. Just as the Sistine Madonna was his regular measurement for beauty, so Lovelace provided his standard of gallant devotion. He meant, of course, the cavalier poet and not the seducer of Clarissa Harlowe. But whatever his model for the passions, or the intensity of their love these two modestly brought up, and ardent young people were as likely to fill their letters with descriptions of working-men's gatherings in gas-lit drill halls as with words of passion, and to complete them with such postscripts as 'Please return my Routh's *Rigid Dynamics*'.

The long engagement was shortened by the insistence of the young people. Lord Bowen died in the early summer of 1894 but not before his consent had been gained to their marriage that same year. It took place conventionally enough at All Saints, Ennismore Gardens, on July 3rd and was followed by a sentimental honeymoon in Germany ending at Bayreuth in a torrent of Wagner.

Ethel had her husband's interests and future deeply at heart. But the early marriage undoubtedly interfered with his work and he left the Naval College already a father, but with only second class honours.

There followed a year in rather dismal lodgings at Southsea. Ethel translated Joinville in the intervals of housekeeping. Josiah bicycled in the grey mornings to Portsmouth dockyard for his day's work. It was high thinking and plain living for the young people and the programme of self-improvement described in their letters to his mother fills a lazier generation with awe.

1896 found them back at Elswick, Josiah now in charge of the drawing offices. There were visits to their distinguished friends and relations in the holidays and once, for Josiah at least, a long stay in Italy assisting in a proposed enlargement of Armstrong's shipyard. The project came to nothing, but the stay provided him with an opportunity of studying Roman remains which, with all the correct books in hand, and the expert guidance of an Italian admiral, was fully taken.

In 1897 the Japanese government offered him a three years appointment as Professor of Naval Architecture in Tokyo at a salary of £700 a year, with a house. He wanted to go but Uncle Hamilton doubted whether Armstrong's would smile on another long absence. With a wife, two children, and a third expected, the exchange of three years' interesting adventure against a safe job with prospects seemed folly. For what was perhaps the only time in his life, he played for safety and turned the offer down.

So the years went by, with days of keen work at

Elswick, cheered by the visits of his brothers, Ralph
and Felix, and their Cambridge friends — George and
Charles Trevelyan, Maurice Amos, Ralph Vaughan
Williams — talking philosophy, politics and history.

Apart from these domestic pleasures there were
from time to time interesting business journeys. One
of these took him to Paris, and he enjoyed, with
Ethel, an evening of romantic ravishment at *Cyrano de
Bergerac*, then in its first triumphant run. True to
their custom they added it to the repertory for
declamation, and to the end of his life he never needed
much provocation to launch out into

Roxane, adieu, je vais mourir . . .

Brave men, romantic adventures, war and love and
intrigue — a strange fantasy population for the brain
of a keen and promising naval architect whose evenings were still spent studying philosophy and political
economy with his wife and considering the betterment
of the world.

In the holidays they visited their older distinguished
friends, J. W. Pease, the banker, with his gifted wife
and daughter, Sir George Otto Trevelyan the historian, and Thomas Hodgkin whose *Italy and Her Invaders*
was rolling forth, tome upon tome, to a rightly respectful public.

Sir George Trevelyan was at work on his great book
— *The American Revolution*. He led Josiah and Ethel
into his library and showed them books that had
belonged to his uncle Lord Macaulay, relics and letters
of the distinguished dead. Some of their owners had
stood in that very library.

That night Ethel had a dream. She had found
herself alone in Sir George Trevelyan's library.
Suddenly she became aware of another presence. It

was Charles Darwin. Hot for certainties, even in a dream, 'Oh, Mr. Darwin,' she cried, 'you will know; tell me is there a God?' The august figure shook its head but Ethel, whose command of words did not forsake her in sleep, pursued her point. 'I don't mean an anthropomorphous being,' she said, 'but a spirit of good in the world?' Again Darwin shook his head. 'Tell me, at least, is there a future life?' she cried, but the vision was fast fading, and she awoke, in tears.

It is a touching and revealing dream and it struck Josiah as profoundly as it had done her, when she recounted it. The minds of these young people were set on the future, on the triumph of good in the world; they were also, his particularly, saturated with the honest ambition to live up to the standards set by distinguished forbears. The talk with Sir George Trevelyan in the library had stirred ambitions which were becoming buried in the pleasant life of every day, the happy, humdrum responsibilities of interesting work and a growing family. The only opening for adventure, the appointment in Tokyo, had been rejected.

But in October 1899 the South African War began and in December, with a wave of others, he volunteered. As things fell out it marked the end of his old life, a change in *tempo*, in character and a move towards the realization of many ambitions.

CHAPTER III

SOUTH AFRICA IN WAR AND PEACE

FOR nearly two years, Josiah was a captain in the Elswick Battery, attached to the second cavalry brigade. He has recorded with delight in his memoirs that he rode 2700 miles in eighteen months and mapped in his spare time large tracts of the country. He had that quality of imagination which romanticizes and brightens not only the past but even the present, and war retained for him (even after the prolonged anguish of 1914-18) its fascination and its poetry. His letters home, from this more chivalrous venture as later from the bloody sand-dunes of Gallipoli, vibrated with an almost boyish excitement. He had always enjoyed riding and now had his fill of it; naturally he turned in his correspondence to the member of his family most sympathetic to his tastes, and his sister Cicely seems to have become his favourite correspondent. She was twenty-three years old at the time, beautiful, and a daring rider. 'Dearest Cicely,' he wrote, 'you would have enjoyed being out with us the day before yesterday — that is to say if you had been cavalry. They had a fifteen mile point-to-point and big prizes. I was just trekking along north of the Vaal between Vereeniging and Villiersdorp thinking what a ripping morning it was, when Lister of the 10th dashed up and said that a Boer convoy had been sighted and that if I could give the infantry the slip there would be some fun. However, the fossilized colonel of the Somersets wouldn't see it and so I didn't get in.'

53

In other letters he expressed doubts and anxieties of another kind. 'Tilly never wasted the Palatinate,' he wrote to Frank, 'as we are laying waste this country. It may be necessary but I don't think the British officer is much of a judge . . . Roughly speaking for every house cleared two irreconcilable men with rifles hide in the mountains.'

For the first time he was seeing the coloured romanticism of historical novels and the heroic phrases of history books reproduced in the brutal facts before him, and he did not always like it. Later he admitted that he had known moments of nightmare — the ghastly confusion at the drifts, the destruction of oxen and horses. Yet the horrors did not prevent him from enjoying the excitement of managing his battery, the pleasure of hard riding and the exercise of skill. He was delighted when the doctor told him that he was the kind of man who 'could sleep in a marsh and ride in hell,' and flattered if a little dismayed when a wild stallion that had been brought in was described by a grinning sergeant as 'just the mount for the captain' and 'the foaming, screaming, amatory monster' was dragged towards him. But he accepted the challenge and mastered the brute, which he loved best of the many horses he rode in that war, and remembered with affection all his life.

Ethel had managed to sail with him. Arrived in South Africa she found to her annoyance that the authorities would let her go no further than Durban. But she was relentless in her ingenuity and more than once arrived illicitly within reach of the front line for a few hours with her warrior. Only when she found herself pregnant did she, for the child's sake, agree to go home.

It was a time of impassioned argument at home

about the ethics of surrender. Troop trains were being constantly held up by Boer commandos, and English officers, caught without any chance of defending themselves, preferred surrender to certain death. High-minded ladies and gentlemen at home were shocked at this pusillanimous conduct. So, in fact, was Josiah, and in later years, with his preference for the dramatic, he declared that his wife had uttered a Spartan ultimatum, 'Never surrender or never come back to me.' The truth seems to have been rather more human; what Ethel wrote in the only letter of hers which touches on the problem was, 'My nightmare is that you and your guns should fall into an ambush and be taken. It would be dreadfully hard to bear. I know you wouldn't do anything so stupid though, and if you did of course I should have to forgive you.'

He was nettled by her contemplating this eventuality at all. 'You really needn't be nervous about my surrendering,' he wrote. 'I have far too much sense of honour to condescend to it for a moment and have satisfied myself that I always have sufficient physical courage to see me through. Do you think it would be a little thing to deserve your contempt?' His courage, which seemed to his friends then and later, an innate characteristic was, in his own view, the result of training. 'I have often been under fire,' he wrote, later in life. 'Never under such circumstances have I not been afraid, but I have always been more afraid of showing it. All our standards are set by what is expected of us.'

If the coming baby was a boy, it was to be 'Victor', but it turned out rather tactlessly to be a girl. 'Humanity forbids "Boadicea",' wrote Ethel, and they settled on Camilla, after the warrior maiden of the *Aeneid*.

Meanwhile, recollecting his pleasure in stirring poetry, Ethel sent him a pocket edition of the spirited patriot Béranger, and, to keep his French from rusting, some novels by George Sand. She also sent him verses of her own composition. 'Colonel Lovelace isn't in it with "The Absent Lovers",' he wrote, delighted.

In May 1901 the war was, to all intents, at an end and the Elswick battery went home. But Josiah had already decided to stay. He was in love with the country, its colours, its mountains, its distances, and its people. He believed in its future and in the possibility of creating lasting peace and understanding between its peoples, white and coloured, now that the war was over. In March he had written to ask Lord Milner whether there would be any place for him in the new administration. The answer was discouraging; there was nothing at the moment but Lord Milner would 'keep him in mind'. Disconsolate, he sailed for home.

II

Josiah did not stay long at home, for he found that conditions had altered at Elswick in his absence and the secure future on which he had counted was no longer promised. He was probably in any case averse to settling down again after his taste of adventure. He had left his heart behind him, and after four months of an uneasy and half-hearted struggle to resume the old life he wrote again to Lord Milner, who had been in England all that summer recruiting his famous 'Kindergarten' of keen young administrators. It was evident that a great experiment in reconstruction and reconciliation was to be conducted as soon as the details of compensation were agreed on, the guerrilla fighting ceased and peace was fully restored. 'I shall be very glad to get men of your stamp,' wrote Milner, 'and I have no doubt that if you were on the spot I could place you before long . . . my experience is that there is never want of places for good men, but great scarcity of good men for places.'

He needed no stronger encouragement, but at once resigned his position at Elswick, handed over his two younger children to his mother and in March 1902 sailed for South Africa with his wife and the three eldest. After eight weeks of anxiety in Cape Town Milner's word came. Just as the Peace of Vereeniging was being signed Josiah was appointed Resident Magistrate for the districts of Ermelo and Carolina. Suddenly doubtful of his capacities, he protested that he knew no law. Lord Milner reassured him and gave him some hints on government in a parting conversation over dinner. He came away inspired and sure of himself. Of Milner he wrote to his mother after this talk, 'I simply love him,' and of himself. 'Can you really imagine my dear Mother, anything in this world that would suit me better.' He had been in Ermelo during the war, riding in on a February night of sousing rain and cold; in a letter home he had described the Vaal near by as 'about the same size and colour as the Trent at Barlaston'. It was the only feature of the landscape which at all recalled his home. The town at which he and his family arrived after a three-day trek from Middelburg, in six wagons and an old ambulance, was as dead and roofless as Pompeii and a good deal more deserted. He had with him, besides his wife and three children, a revenue clerk, some massive handbooks on the law, and supplies for three months.

The district under his care was the size of Wales, inhabited by about 40,000 people of whom 30,000 were natives. He faced the task of rebuilding a war-broken society with a not unnatural anxiety. Soon he was writing to his brother Ralph:

Dear Ralph,

I am in an exceedingly interesting position — only it is too much for me to cope with. Imagine the most ruined town in a ruined country, where anything ordered takes a month to arrive at the railway station and then sticks till you can get casual transport over the next sixty miles; where everybody is ruined financially except for enormous outstanding debts, which cannot be recovered for five months from now.

The one important question is what compensation will they give us and when will it be paid. When they burnt this town, they burnt principally English property — not to mention the government property. Watson had just completed his hotel — £8000. It went aloft before his eyes — so did the English stores and all the English houses — and now they won't come back.

It is two months since the war ended and not only is no rebuilding begun, but no material is ordered to begin with. Can you imagine a town with no wood except from packing cases, no nails, and no intercourse with the outer world, except a casual man on a bicycle from Standerton? And with some dozen inhabitants who can do nothing but rig up a fancy iron shelter and twirl their thumbs.

So far as the district is concerned — reconstruction is rather better; the Boer is more self-sufficing and can get on without money in a small way. Their transport is as usual the difficulty. What animals remain alive require feeding and there is no grass and no forage.

The points that principally vex me in their regard are the continual demand for food when there is no food, and when you can't believe them; and the question of the native. The native holds his land on the feudal system by right of labour. As he has for two years enjoyed his land *and* £2 10s. od. a month and rations — he objects now to working for nothing at the orders of the returned Boer. But he has got to. The complication of the Boer evicting and robbing the native who has helped us is also a very fruitful source of trouble.

Everybody — myself especially — is waiting and longing for the repatriation depot, which at some golden date is going to blossom forth here and sell everything at cost price, and give it away if necessary.

I have had no 'cases' so far. A talking-to generally does it, which is lucky as there is no prison.

Ethel does all the cooking admirably and it would be just heavenly if I could only get a letter occasionally and it wasn't so cold at night. . . .

At present I feel like offering everybody money on loan if they will only start something, but I know all they will say is: 'I will wait and see what compensation I get and then perhaps prices will be lower.'

Little by little the burghers who had been on commando to the end of the war began to reappear. Two English doctors came. The Bank and the Post Office were set up in tents, but often they bore the notice 'Closed for rounders'. Rounders can be played without elaboration; any ball and any stick will do; the course marks itself. Memories of games on Barlaston lawn must have come back, and rounders was instituted as the first popular recreation of Ermelo. Social evenings under canvas with riotous games of 'Up Jenkins' soon followed. Later a sail spread on the square did for a dance floor, until Josiah ordered a wooden one from Durban and inaugurated it with a masked ball. There were weekly lectures, lecturers being found among the inhabitants and the Magistrate's staff. Literary, philosophic political debates followed, then Shakespeare readings, open to all, organized by Ethel. The 'Residency tents' — with little furniture and an erratic food supply became the social cultural centre of the district. The Resident Magistrate kept open house under canvas. A bare fortnight after his arrival a newspaper was issued, produced on the office mimeograph, and called the *Repatriot*; later it became the *Highveld Herald*.

Josiah was always in the saddle, riding from end to end of the district. Half his task was assessing claims and issuing compensation in cash and kind. The other half was reconciling the Afrikaans-speaking population to the new government. He liked the Boers and they liked him; the Puritanism of these Calvinist farmers, whose literature was the Bible and whose historic traditions were those of Dutch independence, appealed to him strongly. He, too, had learnt the Bible young and been reared on Motley. In Capetown he had collected four volumes containing the pedigrees of the Boer settlers down to the time of the Great Trek. Genealogy, whether his own or anyone else's, already asserted its peculiar fascination over him. He carried the books round from shattered farmstead to farmstead, got them out, traced their owners back to their origins. 'Provide a man with a pedigree,' he said, 'and he will never remain your enemy'; a generalization which, in spite of the inverted snobbishness of our time, remains amazingly true. He added another reflection which he had probably learnt from the novels of Sir Walter Scott, for it is not an idea native to English soil: 'Call men by the name of their land and you confer aristocracy.' He conferred it and was popular.

From the account which he wrote in his memoirs it would seem to have been a period of unadulterated hope and energetic effort. His memory of places as of people always took the impress of what was gay, glorious and hopeful. The rest would be blurred away. Passages in some of his letters and the recollections of other people piece together a picture of hard, laborious, and often dispiriting toil. But there were great compensations. He enjoyed the open air life and the riding. Before breakfast he would go for a gallop with his wife and some of the children. 'We are without doubt the happiest family party in the Transvaal,' he wrote to Cicely, describing these occasions. It was fun, as he told her, to go driving over the country in a wagon drawn by four horses 'spinning through water and over the veldt when you don't quite know when a three-foot rut or an ant-bear hole will land you in the heather'. It was fun, when leisure permitted, simply to sit in the sun and watch his horses grazing. He was proud of them, and delighted when Ethel rode one of them to victory at a local race meeting.

His sister Cicely was, of all his family, still his favourite correspondent. It was to her that he wrote a description of the patriarchal wedding-feast on a Boer farmstead:

I owe you a long letter, so that I had better give you an account of the Schalk Meyer marriage. In a succession of Cape Carts over the veldt went I and my clerk. It was 30 miles and we outspanned at the Vaal. Soon after things began to liven. At each farm we passed, a wedding party was getting ready, for Schalk Meyer blind and voiceless is the King of New Scotland with 50,000 acres of his own. Then the wedding corteges began to sweep past us. They habitually move at a gallop. 'loos Smit driving 6 mules covered with ribbands, Barend Smit, J.P. and ex-Veldtcornet, with a flying Cape Cart wildly challenging me to a Cape Cart race on the day of the races (next Saturday), et hoc genus omne. . . .

First we entered the wagon house — a windowless erection with an iron roof laid on tree trunks. Then the antenuptial contract was duly signed. Then we adjourned to another large but stuffy chamber, with a table in the middle and opposite three pairs of chairs draped in white and covered with coloured strings of paper which adhered to and marked the happy couples for many hours. The wedding took place at 12 noon. They all crowded in till the place was like the Black Hole. First old Schalk and his wife were turned off then his son Capt. Meyer, then his daughter-in-law who married our Caspar Badenhorst. I was not quite prepared for this. Only the day before I had sent a particular message out to this young gentleman to tell him that I considered him a 'coward and a blackguard'. He had had a sort of fight with Bothema (hands upper),[1] which, Bothema being drunk — had resulted in his being knocked down first blow, whereafter Badenhorst sat on his chest and pounded his head into a jelly while he lay unconscious. Unfortunately Bothema had begun the row and couldn't complain.

The ceremony over, Barend Smit took a select party round the place which had been the scene of a somewhat exciting dawn fight . . . Ben Smit is a gentleman and a great friend of mine. His sister was there in a Parisian costume. She was fresh from Pretoria where things are a little *difficile*. We had a wordy warfare in which the shortcomings of the British from every point of view were met in a spirit of banter which finally floored the young lady to the great enjoyment of her family. Then at last came dinner . . . My plate was insistently plied with course after course one on top of the other. When I had worked down far enough through a course I called for more which went on top. Being old campaigners we got the red liquorice — wine of New Scotland — changed for a surreptitious bottle of whisky under the table.

---

[1] 'hands upper' – the opprobrious term used by the irreconcilable Boer for those who had capitulated sooner.

Somehow we wiled away the afternoon . . . The time
was broken by a special meeting with Caspar Badenhorst
which rapidly became a public function. In my best judicial
manner I told him what I thought of him and why, ending
with 'I'll modify my opinion of you when you have a fair
stand up fight with Bothema and I'll be there to see fair
play'. The Boers are singularly amenable to reason and
they fairly cheered. The other interview was with Schalk
Meyer. They rudely call him a 'dopper' and a 'takkard' and
I had to persuade him to let us have the dance there instead
of adjourning to an adjoining farm on account of his religious
scruples. Finally he agreed to retire to the wagon house out
of range of the concertina. He is reputed never to have
taken off his clothes. Certain it is that he never removed
them or his top hat all that night. When I left at 5.30 next
morning he and his wife were still sitting in high backed
chairs in the wagon house like old Egyptian kings. You see
there wasn't anywhere to sleep. I had a bedroom prepared
for me. I found 8 Boers sitting on the bed consuming gin.
Later we played whist and later still the room was occupied
by the ladies, while the bedding was piled in another room
for me. Though they offered to have an eviction of the
various people sleeping all over this latter room — children
from 8 years upwards — I declined with thanks. The dancing
began about 4.30 p.m. About 5.30 I put my head in to have
a dance with Miss Smit. The atmosphere was unbreathable
and I fled. There were some hundred couples dancing on
linoleum in a room 30 × 15. All night long the fiddle and
concertina played the same tune. Each dance was the same
— the common schottische. Each lasted 2 minutes with an
interval of 30 seconds while they walked round. How they
managed to dance and breathe in that atmosphere for 12
solid hours I don't know. They hardly ever came out, and
they were still dancing at 5.30 a.m. when I left. The fiddle
has broken down and the concertina was patched all round
with handkerchiefs. So I and the respectables played whist
while boys and girls slept around us on the floor. . . . About
12 I decided to sleep somewhere and curled up in my Cape

Cart. I was discovered, however, by Badenhorst and young Meyer who insisted on my taking a feather bed under Badenhorst's wagon. So I slept as one does when each moment dogs, kaffirs and children came rushing past one's head. I heard many interesting conversations that night, but when it came to the newly wed ones going to bed in the wagon 2 feet over my head I thought I had better sleep.

This is rather long. Over our voyage to Amsterdam with Helen[1] and what befell there I shall have to draw the veil of oblivion, although mighty deeds were done to pacify the districts.

Ethel and her Home Reading union are now the chief weapon of harmony. There is no such district as the district of Ermelo and peace reigns in the land.

In the autumn of 1902 Uncle Hamilton had died at the age of fifty-nine. The £200,000 which he left to his sister Emily and her sons was a godsend to Josiah. He realized his shares in Armstrong's and brought his whole fortune to South Africa. The income, with his salary as Resident Magistrate, was substantial; he put it all into the job. The Ermelo hotel, which its proprietor had watched go aloft in flames, was rebuilt to house a growing number of visitors. His house, and before that his tents, stood hospitably open to all manner of guests. The wooden dance floor must have come from this source, too, and the funds with which, all over the district, clubs and libraries were founded. His straightforwardness and energetic goodwill made him popular and he was to be remembered in South Africa long after he left. Among the younger men working with him at this time two at least rose to considerable distinction — Colonel W. R. Collins who was later Minister for Agriculture in the Union government and Louis Esselen, father of the United Party and political adviser to General Smuts.

[1] His eldest daughter, aged seven.

At first it had been benevolent despotism. Josiah enjoyed that, and never, all his days, made a secret of it. He liked the patriarchal life, whether at home with his family at Barlaston or in his tents on the veldt. Generations of puritan ancestry warmed his blood to this Old Testament patriarchy. His political convictions were, of course, of quite a different colour. Local government was being introduced, municipal offices built. The registration of land and the fixing of rates was going forward. Josiah had not yet read *Progress and Poverty* and become a disciple of Henry George. But his brother Ralph, writing from home, urged him to have the rates levied on land value alone. He seems, therefore, at this time to have been merely acting on an indirect knowledge of the gospel according to Henry George, which was later to become of such importance in his life. The land registration and the rating were indirectly based on this economic doctrine, and the system worked well. The serious disappointment which Josiah had at this time was of a different kind. He had hoped for universal municipal suffrage; it was not granted. Indians (and of course Kaffirs) were excluded. From this exclusion, he always believed, the yet unsolved troubles of South Africa have all come.

Eighteen months of devoted and energetic work had, however, laid the foundations of prosperity and understanding at Ermelo. The district was also, as the benevolent despot happily realized, being nourished in the traditions of critical democracy in which he believed. Its newspaper, the *Highveld Herald*, had at first held a careful balance between the British government and the anti-British Boers; it was not, to start with, successful. This was a pity since it was the only organ of public opinion and propaganda. Josiah

dissociated it from the government, set it up independently with a new editor, and let it crackle with
abusive articles about his person and his administration. Sometimes he composed the attacks himself:
'There are few things I enjoy more than writing
leaders slanging myself,' he wrote to Ralph. The
result was gratifying. The paper went with a swing
and became popular at once. It was a trick, but a
trick on the right lines, for it established among the
people the idea of a democracy, based on the fearless-
ness of the governed and their right to criticize. Un-
happily, just as things were going well, the editor, an
attractive irresponsible, decamped. After that Josiah
sold the *Highveld Herald*, now fully established, to
Boer owners. Since then it has become an organ of
the Nationalist party, *Het Volk*, and the subsequent
record of the *Hoogeveld Herald* disappointed the high
hopes of understanding, union and equality of all
men with which its first editor ran off its earliest
numbers on a mimeograph in a tent.

After eighteen months he felt that life and warmth
had come back to the district. But he watched with
anxiety the increase of national prejudices: 'Both sides',
he wrote home, 'are drawing the race-line tight and
we shall have boycotting soon as merrily as in Cape
Colony.' His well-founded anxieties on the political
future in South Africa were, however, soon to be
submerged by a domestic anxiety which altered the
course of his career.

A little more than a year after his arrival the new
Residency was at last completed. Covering the last
stage of the journey by ox-cart, the familiar furniture
and books arrived from England: framed photographs
of Bellini's 'Doge' and the family of Josiah Wedgwood I
disporting on their lawn; Kinglake, Macaulay,

Motley's *Dutch Republic* and the *Memoirs of Marbot* — all
of them symbols that South Africa was now his home,
the place in which he had set up his household gods.

Then quite suddenly Ethel was taken ill. Neither
of the doctors in Ermelo could find anything wrong,
yet her illness appeared to be as grave as it was
mysterious. Josiah applied for six months leave and
took her first to the coast, and, when this did not seem
to help, back to England. The visit to England
apparently cured her, and they set out once more, but
at Grand Canary, after a rough crossing, she refused
to go any further. He could, of course, have gone on
alone, leaving her to follow. But he was convinced,
then and ever after, that she would not do so, that the
choice before him was between his career and his
wife. For this reason, thinking of his family as well as
of his wife, he cabled his resignation and turned back
to England.

For the second time his chosen path had come to an
abrupt end. He had turned his back on his prospects
as a naval architect to follow a career of adventure,
whence he had turned towards a life of service in a
country with which he had fallen in love. Now, at
thirty-two, he came back to England with no plans
and no future.

CHAPTER IV

EARLY YEARS IN
PARLIAMENT

I N England he sought advice from his brother
Ralph,[1] then working at York with the North-
Eastern Railway. They talked economics and
politics, discussed the experiment in the taxation of
land which Josiah had tried at Ermelo, and the works
of Henry George. He had time on his hands for
reading and began to study *Progress and Poverty* in
detail. The basic doctrine of Georgian economics is
that all wealth derives from land, which should be free
to all, and could be made so if taxation were simplified
to a single tax on the site value of land, thus forcing
proprietors to put it to its full use or to sell it to those
who were ready to do so. 'If men cannot find an
employer,' wrote Henry George, 'why can they not
employ themselves? Simply because they are shut out
from the element on which human labour can alone
be exerted; men are compelled to compete with each
other for the wages of an employer, because they have
been robbed of the natural opportunities of employing

[1] My father is to figure so often in this book in the part of counsellor and
friend as well as younger brother that this seems a convenient place to give a
few more details. On leaving Cambridge he had entered the service of the
North-Eastern Railway company. During the first world war he was Director
of Docks in France and after the war General Manager of the North-Eastern
Railway. When the multitudinous British railways were grouped he became
Chief General Manager of the London and North-Eastern Railway and at the
outbreak of the second world war was chairman of the Railway Executive
Committee. In 1942 he was created a baronet; there was some discussion
between him and Josiah, who had become a peer at the same moment, as to the
territorial designation appropriate to each of them. Josiah decided to be 'of
Barlaston', the village of his birth, and relinquished to my father the addition
'of Etruria', which one or other of them had decided to take in remembrance
of the name of old Josiah's original Works.

themselves; because they cannot find a piece of God's world on which to work without paying some other human creature for the privilege.'

The doctrine had been born in America when the westward thrust of civilization and cultivation was still vigorously progressing across an undeveloped continent. *Progress and Poverty* appeared in 1880, the best known book among the colossal output of Henry George, who wrote and spoke with undiminishing vigour from 1868 until his death in 1897. His writing, like that of his compatriot Edward Bellamy, is full of generous warmth and eloquent indignation against existing conditions. He has been described as an inspired mutineer, whose rebellion grew from religious and humanitarian roots. Complacency of all kinds fanned his indignation and gave to it such a gale of words that — alike in England and America — he took readers and audiences by storm. In 1904, when Josiah came back to England, the Georgian doctrine was fast gaining ground.

Josiah accepted the doctrines of Henry George and maintained them to the end of his life; he also fell in love with the character and the language of the prophet. He liked the heat and colour of the writing and absorbed phrases and paragraphs into his vocabulary of argument. He liked, indeed he loved, the integrity and the generosity of the writer, and in his *Memoirs* nearly forty years later he paid tribute to the man who was undoubtedly the greatest single influence on his ideas.

From those magnificant periods, unsurpassed in the whole of British literature, I acquired the gift of tongues. Ever since 1905 I have known that there was a man from God, and his name was Henry George! I had no need thenceforth for any other faith.

The tribute should not be regarded as considered literary criticism, but it reflects, with characteristic and sincere exaggeration, the place of Henry George in Josiah's personal Pantheon of the illustrious dead.

Henry George shone as a beacon of hope on Josiah's clouded and narrowing horizon. Here he was back in England, without a job, without a future, frustrated of his career in South Africa and looked on with a hint of disapproval by his steady-going relations in and around the Wedgwood Works. After all it was the second career he had thrown up.

In those days, however, the £ was still worth twenty shillings and his private means were sufficient to support his family. He took the eighteenth-century house, Barlaston Hall, a few hundred yards from where his mother still lived at the Lea. It is a beautiful house. A graceful double staircase of faded brick sweeps up to a broad terrace, on to which open the long windows of the great saloon. The house is solid, nobly proportioned, echoing far-off memories of Italian baroque in its gentlemanly Georgian. The garden, laid out on the Italian model, has to this day the flower beds planned two hundred years ago, each surrounded by a low stone curb to keep its outline clear. Inside, the doors have carved pediments, broken with baskets of fruit and cornucopias and touched with faded colours. The staircase, running round a wide square well and surmounted by a little cloister-like gallery of panelled arches on slender double columns, is cantilevered out from the wall and runs up three floors without supports. This, Josiah calculated, might have done very well for ladies in panniers moving sedately from floor to floor, but what would happen when five rampageous children pounded up and down? It could not possibly be safe.

The builders told him it was; but he insisted on reinforcing the structure with wooden joists, still known locally as Wedgwood's Folly. But Josiah was not only an anxious father; he was a trained engineer. He said the staircase was no longer safe, and in fact he was right.

Later he bought a patch of land on a steep damp hill-side about three miles off and built a house of his own — a wooden bungalow on the South African model. This new home was long, low, neat and un-obtrusive, coated with brown creosote and lit by large windows at regular intervals; it had a large veranda, and was surmounted by a tarred roof. It has a very large living room and a surprising number of smaller rooms — so many that newcomers sometimes got lost inside it. It is convenient but lacks architectural elegance; on the other hand it can absorb an in-definite number of inmates. Under its unassuming roof, through decades of distress and war, many were the outcasts who were to find refuge: conscientious objectors between terms of imprisonment, Indian agitators, Balkan liberals, stranded enemy aliens, refugee Jews and Social Democrats, the children of fathers dead or dying in Nazi concentration camps, the persecuted and the disconsolate of three generations and many lands. He called his house Moddershall Oaks, but everyone else called it 'the Ark'. The name was appropriate to its neat toy-shop appearance, but, through the years, it became touchingly suitable to this tiny ship of refuge riding the political storm.

The pleasure which Josiah took in being reunited to his family was some comfort for what he had lost in South Africa. They were the poorer by the loss of his only sister Cicely; she had married and left for India with her husband just before he came back from South Africa. A few months later she died at Poona, leaving to her brothers the undimmed recollection of a youth and beauty that time would now never fade.

Meanwhile, the youngest brother, Felix, had grown up and provided for the moment a scintillating focus of family interest and speculation. He was a passionate and already a distinguished mountaineer, although he did not make his dangerous and solitary attempt on the highest peak in the Andes until a year or two later. But it was his literary talent which delighted the family; he wrote verse — serious poems in a Meredithian manner, and lighter poems indiscriminately in French and English in an entertaining and skilful satirical-bombastic vein; he had ideas on writing, on prose and plot and style, went about much with his Cambridge friend Desmond MacCarthy ('a dark young Irishmen', wrote Ethel, 'who believes he can make a living by literature'), and was clearly determined on an Elizabethan career of mingled action and creation.

In Staffordshire, too, Josiah found a ready-made position which ministered to his shaken self-confidence. 'It is something new to find oneself effusively welcomed simply for the name one bears. I might be an idiot or a pauper,' he wrote to Ralph, 'but to be called Josiah Wedgwood is a claim to distinction I never grasped before and I like it very much.' He sought to justify the name by entering immediately into local affairs. Ethel's new obsession was temperance, and he soon found himself addressing the local Temperance Club, although he used the occasion sometimes for other subjects and spoke with eloquence and feeling on the 'iniquitous' practice of docking horses' tails. But although ready to champion the noblest of beasts, he

73

had had to give up riding. His finances no longer allowed him to keep a horse and he adapted himself, with typically romantic enthusiasm, to the bicycle.

History also claimed him and while Ethel went back to her old task of translating Joinville, he became immersed in local and family history. He joined the local antiquarian society, the William Salt Society, and was soon announcing to Ralph with pardonable pride that he had found the earliest recorded Wedgwood. The father of the line was lowly born, a 'villein-virgater' in the year 1308 and apparently in some trouble with the law. This ancestry suited Josiah the rebel very well.

He needed some ancestral support, for the dominating members of his own family, his mother and the uncle and cousin who, with his eldest brother Frank, now reigned at the Etruria Works, were stalwart Conservatives. But the times stirred with Revolution and his heart with them.

Isn't the news from Petersburg soul-stirring? [he wrote to Ethel during a short absence in London, where he had read the papers full of the famous December riots of 1904.] Revenge, starvation and a good cause should make short work of the autocrat and his detestable gang. If only the Russians had half the pluck of the French the paving stones would have risen of themselves and we should see a 'feast of pikes'. *Et tous les ponts du Neva seront jonchés de cadavres* — as a fine poet[1] puts it. I only hope my sons will some day wear the red cap of liberty for my fighting days are over and even you will strike at a trip to Siberia and the role of Louise Michel.[2]

Less stirring events nearer home gave him some

[1] The quotation is from a bombastic poem by his brother Felix of which I can only supply one other line, the first, *En avant la Pologne*.
[2] This Parisian governess, heroine of the Commune, was a favourite with him.

personal anxiety. He knew that his brother Frank and
cousin Cecil did not altogether like his connections
with the local Liberal Club. He addressed meetings
at which, as he reported to Ralph, he said what he
thought of the more burning problems of the day.
'Does it sound to you improper?' he asks, with touching faith that his younger brother, the 'wary-wise
Odysseus' of nursery days, would advise him in the
delicate task of reconciling conscience with family
duty.

This letter was written on February 4th, 1905;
nine days later he had more significant news.

> I want your support badly [he wrote to Ralph]. I
> have news. The Liberal candidate for Newcastle [under-
> Lyme] has retired and the idea is that I should be selected to
> take his place. Of course it is serious, but it is only by taking
> risks that I have done anything so far, and I have determined
> to go in for it. There will be a meeting on Thursday of the
> Liberal 500. I know you will agree with me as to this step,
> but at times I feel horribly low about the expense, though I
> know perfectly well that I can afford it. Frank and mother
> too will make a fearful fuss. I wish it were you not me . . .
> Will you write to Frank and tell him he must support me . . .
> Won't you stand too? We might do something together.

Soon afterwards, the local press announced the
adoption of the new Liberal candidate who was described as an earnest student of public affairs command-
ing the personal respect of the entire community. He
was also described as an excellent speaker of free and
forcible views. Whatever the impression he made, he
still found public speaking very difficult. 'If I could
acquire the tongue of Demosthenes with the same ease
that I shall acquire the seat of Sir Alfred Haslam [the
sitting Conservative member] I should indeed be

blessed', he lamented. Eagerly he swallowed praise for his strenuous efforts. Ethel was immensely busy with suggestions and ideas. Once when she had written the speech which he had learnt by heart, his audience of Young Liberals declared they had heard nothing like it since Gladstone. 'Ethel was pleased', he recorded with charming ingenuousness.

Meanwhile, family disapproval rumbled round the horizon. His cousin Cecil, the influential chairman of Josiah Wedgwood & Sons, told the local Conservative Club that the family did not support the rebel and regretted the use to which its name and prestige were being put. Josiah was indignant and it needed all the diplomacy of his genial and generous eldest brother Frank to prevent an open quarrel.

Meanwhile, the gathering unrest in the country rocked the uneasy Unionist government. Demands for reform, for land tenure based on small holdings, for the abolition of the Lords and a fiscal policy of cheap food swelled the Liberal sails. In December 1905 Mr. Balfour resigned, Sir Henry Campbell-Bannerman succeeded as Prime Minister and, recognizing the temper of the times, immediately appealed to the country.

The Conservative *débâcle* and the sweeping Liberal triumph of January 1906 followed. The North Staffordshire Conservative seats fell like a house of cards, Newcastle-under-Lyme among them. The slogan was 'Free Trade. Free Land. Free Breakfast Table'. The schoolchildren marched about the frosty streets to the invigorating chorus of 'Stamp, stamp, stamp upon Protection', and Josiah preached the Georgeite doctrine from his platform. The Conservative candidate drove solemnly to his meetings in a carriage and pair. It was only another sign of the times when the Liberal candidate came jerking along in a back-firing motor car.

To the last the family was divided, taking its quarrel as humorously as it could. The older generation of aunts was especially puzzled, some warming to old libertarian traditions, others conservative as only old libertarians can be. 'Rumour has it that Aunt Amy has paired with Cousin Snow, but Cousin Caroline and Cousin Effy refuse to pair on moral grounds.' So Josiah informed Ralph of the noddings and exclamations in the family parlours.

After the count on the night of his victory Josiah saw Ralph off by the midnight train to the north from Stoke-on-Trent. Dark and cold between the gas lamps loomed the statue of old Josiah on his pedestal. With one accord the brothers scrambled up it and crowned the decorous eighteenth-century head with the blue ribbon of Liberalism. In the morning it was taken down on the instant order of the indignant head of the family.

II

The two Staffordshire papers re-acted typically to the Liberal victory at Newcastle. The liberally disposed *Evening Sentinel* patted the victor on the head as 'a young man of great energy and engaging personality'. The Conservative *Staffordshire Advertiser* sneered at the 'incompetent, badly-dressed, well-to-do person, who thanks to the blindness of the English voters won a seat in Parliament'.

Newcastle-under-Lyme, the borough which Josiah was to represent for the next thirty-five years, is an ancient city, with a royal charter issued by King Henry II. It has been returning members to Parliament since Parliament began and counted among its citizens several historic names. Josiah was always very well pleased to remember among them Thomas Harrison, the Puritan soldier and Republican, who had opposed alike the authoritarian governments of Charles I and Cromwell and died on the gallows, with notable constancy, for the 'good old Cause'. In similar circumstances Josiah would have done much the same and with as good a heart.

Causes, old or new — but in the end there is only one cause, an old one, that of justice — were to be the speciality of the member for Newcastle-under-Lyme. The representative whom the borough continued to return to Parliament for the next eight elections was to have a stormy career; he was to change his party allegiance, to navigate the muddy rapids of a much publicized divorce, to figure in the newspapers repeatedly in the guise of trouble-maker and irresponsible, to wander far afield in the quest for justice to Indians, Russians and Jews. But he never ceased to be at heart a Staffordshire man, a true son of the pot-bank, steeped in local tradition, sympathetic to local loyalties, the first to speak and the best informed on the conditions and interests of the workers in the potteries, and a determined advocate of the rights and dignity of the ancient borough of Newcastle-under-Lyme. He was twice mayor.

At the time of his election, and on the threshold of his third and last career, that of politics, he was thirty-four years old. At this time his pictures show a tall, uncouth, energetic man with a fiercely drooping moustache and heavy eyebrows. He was not classically handsome, but attractive, with his fine grey eyes and outjutting jaw. His appearance was dominating and his voice resonant, and he contrived to seem (although

78

he was not yet) a ready speaker. The *Advertiser* had spoken no more than the truth about his clothes. Etiquette in 1906 made a top-hat *de rigueur* in the House of Commons (James Keir Hardie alone represented Merthyr in a deer-stalker) but apart from the top-hat Josiah's attire was liable to be incorrect. His movements and his way of walking, between a swagger and a slouch with long, loping strides, wrecked the sit of any suit. He used pockets to put things in, including his hands. He liked odd materials and odd colours; later his buff waistcoat became well known; once he sported a velvet jacket as though he were a painter from Chelsea; certainly the first time I remember him he was wearing a bottle green coat with bright metal buttons. (I was struck dumb with admiration.) Not that these oddities went so far as eccentricity, nor did he cultivate them as a pose. What he cultivated — for after all some personal peculiarity, be it a pipe, or umbrella or cigar, must be cultivated to help the cartoonists — what he cultivated was his jaw. It had always been prominent; thrusting it well out to emphasize his arguments, which were many, he soon made it the most striking feature of his face.

But it was his smile which won hearts. It was an exceptionally charming one and perfectly natural, much more truly characteristic than the determined chin. It had above all the quality of being directly related to the person who had caused it; it was not a pleasant, automatic social response, but a spontaneous expression of real delight of which the person to whom it was directed was the unique, amazing and special cause. It was the most flattering smile I have ever known.

However *gauche* he had been in youth and early manhood, he had by this time acquired a charm, which the years developed into one of his surest weapons. Indignant dowagers and crusted colonels who got into his company somehow by error, thinking him little less than Antichrist, thawed into genial streams of small talk under his sunshine. He was particularly good with women, although in the early days his sincere but incurably romantic gallantry was too stilted to meet all occasions. The simple rule that a woman does not like to look her age does not always hold; his children record with delight his absent-minded response to a younger daughter who had announced with pride that she would be five to-morrow: 'I assure you, my dear, you don't look it.' The lamentable howl which greeted this, taught him wisdom, for when I was twelve he expressed the most tactful amazement; he had taken me for quite four-teen. Trivialities, but significant of that kindly desire to please which is the innocent cause of much happiness in the world.

These were the superficialities. The fundamental characteristics were unalterable honesty of purpose, resolute courage, and a ferociously active and inquiring mind. Despising compromise, expediency, and half-measures, he went into Parliament for the righting of wrongs, the protection of the oppressed, the exposure of injustice; also, and above all, to establish the millennium by the taxation of land values.

III

In the autumn of 1905, on his visits to London, Josiah had seen a good deal of his old Northumberland friends, the Walter Runcimans. Runciman had come down to speak for him during his campaign; when he became Financial Secretary to the Treasury Josiah was appointed his Parliamentary Private Secretary. Almost immediately he proved himself rather too unorthodox for this part; not that Walter Runciman had been so unwise as to expect conventional behaviour from him, on the contrary he was from the first very willing to overlook Josiah's displays of independent judgment. Although a staunch member of the Liberal party, nothing was further from Josiah's conception of his duty to his constituents and his conscience than the idea of a slavish obedience on all questions. While faithful to his party on the larger issues, he judged independently and acted independently on every question that merited or attracted his attention. His maiden speech was one of the few occasions when he deviated from this rule and characteristically he hated the recollection of it. The question was a South African one: should measures protecting the native population from uncontrolled exploitation be included in the projected new constitution for the Transvaal? Josiah, on the Government side, found himself defending a policy of non-intervention. He was able to argue with some conviction against legislative interference in general and to say with truth that in his experience he had seen no ill-treatment of Kaffir workers. But the very brief speech has an air of half-heartedness quite foreign to his usual character. He was in two minds and wished afterwards he had not spoken. His ambition for South Africa was a constitution based on the enfranchisement of all inhabitants, white, native and coloured. Had such a franchise been established special protection for the Kaffirs might not be necessary. But he was already becoming aware that true democracy never would be established in South Africa. The problem perturbed him greatly.

As soon as he found his feet in his new surroundings he began to exercise his private judgment, voting against the government whenever his conscience dictated, which was rather too often to be suitable in a P.P.S. Usually the issues were straightforward matters of opinion, but he was sometimes swayed by personal loyalties. Milner had recently returned from South Africa where his administration had, in the last years, been strongly criticized. The importing of indentured Chinese labour to work the mines had been vehemently attacked. It was indeed one of the chief issues in the recent election; the violent popular opposition to this twentieth-century form of slavery had played a large part in securing the Liberal victory. Josiah felt strongly about Chinese labour, but he could not forget what he owed to Milner as his old chief, and when a motion of censure was moved against him in the House of Commons he would not vote with the Liberals. Soon afterwards he resigned his position as P.P.S.

Now began his apprenticeship in the art of asking questions. It was Redmond's advice to young members that they should exercise their wits and acquire Parliamentary training by asking as many questions as possible, hardening themselves to the repeated snubs of ministers. Josiah was by no means as fierce as his moustache made him look and the daily exercise of one question and two supplementaries cost him much in nervous anxiety. He used to bet with himself on the number of supplementaries he would achieve in a week. As the moment approached he would run over in his mind the jingle of names which he always used to restore his courage: 'Dutton of Dutton, Delves of Doddington, Hawkstone of Wrinehill, Fowlhurst of Crewe.' These were the four squires of Lord Audley who had performed great deeds with their master on the field of Poitiers. Pursuing his genealogical passion in his spare time, Josiah had traced his descent from at least three of them. The reminder gave him courage and, as he rose in his place, the House of Commons swam with the lances of Froissart.

In season and out of season he advocated the Single Tax as the solution to all problems of unemployment and finance. He spoke on it in Parliament and at public meetings, wrote on it in the press, proselytized among his friends. Winston Churchill stopped him once to say conversationally, 'I've just been reading your Henry George, Wedgwood, and I must say I can't see the catch in it.' A new disciple. 'Thank God!' exclaimed Josiah as he walked on. Later he heard that Churchill's account of the incident, with gesture, tone and upward glance, was causing great amusement. He was distressed, for you should not jest on sacred subjects. Mr. Balfour was kinder; at the end of one of Josiah's determined appeals for the application of the Georgian doctrine he suavely declared that, 'The honourable gentleman deserves praise for his courage in expressing clearly and standing by his eccentric opinions. I am glad to give it.'

On Sundays Josiah was often to be heard addressing an open air crowd on the Single Tax. He shouted from the plinth of Nelson's column; flanked by his two sons he led a procession from the Embankment to Hyde Park.

In 1909 he became the President of the English League for the Taxation of Land Values and seemed to spend most of his time hurrying from place to place eloquently preaching the doctrine. Thus to a fellow-worker in Yorkshire he wrote in a typical letter:

I have been getting in letters, articles, speeches right and left . . . I have been having splendid open-air meetings with trades unionists and such like . . . Bristol, Southampton, Newport, Cardiff, Dartford, North Wales etc. and things are getting pleasantly ripe, though I am not quite certain whether it is the landlords heads or those of the police that will be broke. Go ahead!

This was the time when the Land Song was born, adapted to the tune of 'Marching Through Georgia'.

The land, the land, 'twas God who gave the land,
The land, the land, the ground on which we stand,
Why should we be beggars with the ballot in our hand?
God gave the land to the people.

The land was for all people regardless of race, creed or colour, and the colonial Empire was as proper a place for the exercise of the doctrine of Henry George as the home country. About this time Josiah played an important part on the Northern Nigeria Land Laws Committee. They prepared a report, on the principles of Henry George, setting down in firm and coherent form the basis of a colonial land policy which would enable the native to hold and develop his own land. *The Times* described this document with justice as 'the most far-seeing measure of constructive statesmanship West Africa has ever known'. The legislation based on the report has in fact secured the natives of Nigeria from being turned into a landless proletariat as has happened in so many other primitive communities.

His experience on this committee and his knowledge of conditions in South Africa made him a pioneer champion of native races. Charles Buxton who later became their most famous advocate in the House of Commons owed his first lessons and his inspiration to his association with Josiah.

But he had other interests. He spoke several times on the Workman's Compensation Act and he introduced a new clause into the Children's Bill. This clause, which made it an offence to give alcohol except for medical purposes to a child under five, was successfully carried. Where an evident physical evil was concerned he was at this time prepared to support and even to initiate State interference. The protection of children was much on his mind at the time (he had six of his own), for he asked a number of pertinent questions about private orphanages, the care of children in workhouses and the work of the N.S.P.C.C. Another class of underprivileged in whose fate he interested himself were the women and girls in rescue homes. He suspected 'that sweated labour masqueraded as charity in the laundries and workshops of some of these institutions.

In the famous budget of 1909 Lloyd George initiated extra taxation to meet both the naval re-armament programme and the social services. This was partly done by a tax on Land Values, in Josiah's view a step in the right direction although by no means far enough to satisfy him. The House of Lords, which had consistently blocked the Liberal social programme, now virtually created a constitutional crisis by throwing out the budget. The Liberals appealed to the country. The election of January 1910 was won by the Liberals to the nation-wide singing of the Land Song which had now quite replaced 'Santa Lucia' as Josiah's favourite musical composition. 'On all questions that come up in politics you will find me on the side of Freedom and Justice as I understand them,' he assured his constituents in his election address, a statement that was exactly true. At about this time he was engaged with Ethel on a series of articles for the land reform paper *The Open Road*, which summed up his political beliefs. These were later published in a book, *The Road to Freedom*. It is, generally speaking, a summary of the ideas of Henry George, proclaiming the necessity of Revolution by the reform of land tenure and the introduction of the Single Tax. Its purpose was indicated in a brief prefatory note:

It is the purpose of this book to show that modern civilization is built upon slave labour; that land monopoly is the cause of this slave labour; that when the land is freed, slave labour must cease, and with it so-called civilization; and that if the unreal civilization be thus ended, the real will have a chance to begin, and true development take the place of spurious progress.

He told his children, consistently, that the book was their mother's work. With staunch loyalty, for he was proud of the book, he insisted on this all the more vigorously after the breakdown of their marriage which was now fast approaching. The book is certainly put together with a skill in interlocking logic that was foreign to him; it is also more didactic than his later style. But the intermittent passion and vigour of the writing is recognizably his.

He had been writing a good deal in the last five years and had developed a manner at once trenchant and easy, impressive and colloquial, which rightly pleased editors and which also rather pleased him. But it was his youngest brother Felix who, in this year 1910, blazed up as a comet in the literary heavens, with an astonishing novel, *The Shadow of a Titan,* in which the career of a Latin American dictator is strangely interwoven with a group of English characters. The scene shifts from the English countryside to the government villas of a Latin American city,

86

strange swamps and forests, mountains and prairies. It is immensely long, powerfully inventive, rich in action and humour and poetry, and written in a style which derives from Meredith. It ran into thirteen impressions within a year of publication and was reviewed with enthusiasm. It is a strange book to read now, for the intrigues and machinations of dictatorship with which we have since become familiar, are here set forth with great imaginative powers at a time when no one imagined such things could happen save in remote equatorial America. Its author did not live to fulfil its promise. He was killed in Flanders five years later.

This publication was naturally an event of importance to the whole family, and competed hotly with the election as a subject of conversation.

I V

Soon after the opening of the 1910 Parliament Josiah got himself into an unfortunate scrape. A friend of his, a hot-tempered and impulsive Irish member, Ginnell, was suspended for the session by the Speaker. Josiah, more sympathetic than wise, dashed off a letter of condolence in which he described the Speaker's action as 'certainly not fair'. Ginnell published the letter in an Irish paper where it was seen by a Conservative M.P. who read it aloud in the House. In the still days of 1910 this was headline news. The indiscretion might even have been the end of a hopeful career. Ethel, who had not seen the letter before it was sent, indignantly declared that this was what came of not consulting his wife's superior wisdom. He himself, though well aware of his indiscretion,

87

could think of no defence beyond expressing astonish-
ment that Ginnell should have committed such a
breach of etiquette as to publish a private letter. His
brother Ralph, summoned hurriedly for consultation,
advised him to abandon this or any line of defence
and to apologize with the right measure of humility
and dignity. The advice was sound: everyone knew
that Josiah's good nature outran his discretion, and
most of his fellow-members rated Ginnell's breach of
confidence as a more serious fault than the writing of
the letter. A crowded house punctuated his speech
with cheers, the Speaker magnanimously accepted the
apology, and the *Morning Post*, of all papers, uttered
words of benign approval over the sinner repentant.

Graver conflicts were in the air. The working-class
movements were gathering strength; strikes were increasingly frequent; the forces of reaction were taking
up their positions against the feared revolution, and
the Liberal government, of which Josiah and others
had hoped so much, was sandwiching its social legislation between measures designed to stem the rising
tide of agitation. Over all loomed the shadow of an
aggressive German Empire so that expenditure on
armaments compelled the Liberals to slow down their
social service programme.

Worse than this, growing fear of a controlled and
disciplined Germany drove the Liberal government
to adopt illiberal measures to quell revolt in India and,
not long after, to coerce the recalcitrants in England.
Josiah went at once to the defence of libertarian principles. In a debate on India he first drew attention to
himself with a reckless championship of the then unpopular cause of Indian freedom. But the bitterness
of his speech reflected his growing disillusion with the
cautious Liberals.

It is for Germany to be governed efficiently, he said, but the negation of the rights of the individual inherent in the *Salus populi* theory is one against which the best in English history have protested. It is curious that this English principle is represented and backed today by two socialist members — Ramsay MacDonald and Keir Hardie — while the man behind whom the bureaucrats take shelter is he who was once John Morley.

In the autumn of 1911 the Duke of Abercorn called for the formation of a 'Volunteer Police Force'. This was to be a band of young men from all stations of life who would constitute themselves the guardians of law and order against hooliganism and attacks on property. Such a body, although in theory open to all, would be largely composed of wealthy young men who might, intentionally or unintentionally, fail to distinguish between hooliganism and legitimate forms of working-class protest. This was the epoch in which, it will be remembered, the occupants of the clubs in Piccadilly had caused an ugly and violent scene by jeering at a working-man's procession. The atmosphere was bitter with incomprehension. Such a body as the Duke of Abercorn's — the kind of body which was later in many European countries to be a nucleus of Fascism — had evident dangers. Josiah attacked it with satirical violence in an article in the Left wing *Eye-Witness*, entitled 'The Honorary Strike-breakers'. The force, he pointed out, would be largely made up of 'club loafers' — young men about town with too little to do and not an atom of comprehension for the real injustices against which the strikers might be protesting.

The sport of harrying the turbulent trade unionist is new, and society wants a change of sport occasionally [he wrote]. There is just that spice of danger which really appeals to your true sportsman, not much, of course, for the real police and the Law Courts will see that risks are minimized, but a danger somewhere just between partridge shooting and fox-hunting — a foundation for good stories, the groundwork of an appetite for the next meal.

The *Eye-Witness* was one among many Left papers, Socialist, Fabian, trades union, Co-operative, Anarchist and Syndicalist, which scandalized a middle-class public unused to such forms of expression, and made them feel that excesses such as they associated only with Frenchmen and foreigners might soon be upon them even in unrevolutionary England. There was only a small Labour party in the House, but there was a growing agitation in the country.

Josiah at this time must have known as much about working-class conditions as any other M.P. not himself of the working class. He counted all the Labour men, especially Keir Hardie and Lansbury, among his closest friends. He had worked as a manual labourer at Newcastle-on-Tyne; he knew conditions in the potteries from top to bottom; he had spoken and visited among the London docks. He thought too highly of the intelligence and restraint of British working-class leaders to have any real fear of revolution and he believed in free speech and strong words. He was therefore appalled when the Liberal government turned the screw on the Left wing press and prosecuted Tom Mann for his articles in *The Syndicalist* urging troops not to fire on strikers.

In a letter to the *Daily News* he expressed his views with his usual vigour:

Sir,

This country seems to me to be threatened with a danger so serious as to call for a public remonstrance.

Three men have been imprisoned and two are awaiting trial for taking part in disseminating an opinion with which numbers of men of all politics and religions sympathize. One is under remand for handing to soldiers a leaflet urging them not to fire on their fellow-countrymen; one is sentenced to nine months hard labour and two small printers to six months hard labour for printing the same appeal; the fourth for publicly declaring that he agrees with them, is awaiting trial.

These men are five, but who knows how many will be in prison before the 'crusade' is over, and how many thousand more would be so, too, if they were not cowed into silence?

These men are prosecuted technically for inciting soldiers to disobey orders (orders not yet given). Technically that is their offence. In reality their offence is that they have ventured to question one of the accepted ideas of comfortable society. It is foolish to pretend that their real crime is inciting to mutiny. Unless you forbid soldiers to read and talk you cannot keep them isolated away from such ideas. The trials alone of Crowsley, Bowman and the Bucks must have made the British Army think, more than any letter in a paper they probably never see, or a leaflet handed to them by a modest railway worker on Sunday morning.

The medieval states were wise in suppressing by similar means the circulation in the vulgar tongue of the New Testament. In it, too, men are bidden not to kill.

These leaflets, letter, speech, expressed ideas which are also approved by most non-resisters and by many ordinary citizens who, recalling horrors of past English history, know that the intervention of the military in industrial disputes leads to the futile barbarities of Peterloo. But supposing this Open Letter had contained something glaringly wrong, is that a reason in England for checking the liberty of the Press, of public speech? Who knows what other doctrines may next be called in question! May we only think and speak freely so long as our beliefs tally with the opinion of the authorities? Are we to be bound in a political creed as particular and circumscribed as any 39 Articles of Religion?

The Crown lawyers imagine that they are suppressing agitation by these 'Treason Trials'. In reality, they are creating revolutionaries. For every man who is sentenced under this obsolete Act of 1797 ten men spring up fired with indignation and with fanatical hatred of Government methods.

Those who believe that freedom of speech and writing are vital to any country's health and far outweigh all danger that can come from the utterance of wrong opinion — as well as those who believe that in appealing to soldiers not to shoot working men the prisoners were right — must regard this action of a Liberal government with something of shame and dismay.

He was not alone in these views. The names of John Masefield, H. A. L. Fisher and Bertrand Russell appear with his as signatories to a firm but more measured letter of protest in *The Times*.

On March 25th, 1912, he made in the House of Commons what was, up to that time, the most striking speech of his career. Using his favourite arguments from history he invoked the great names of Sheridan and Fox, Erskine and Horne Tooke in defence of a free Press. 'God forbid,' he said, 'that honest opinion should ever be made a crime . . . I plead with the Government, not in the interests of these men . . . I plead with the Government in the interests of the Liberal traditions of our country, of which we all, on whichever side of the House we sit, are justly and rightly proud.'

The Government soon after dropped the remaining prosecutions. Josiah had himself been much concerned about the case of Fred Crowsley, the 'modest railway worker' of his *Daily News* letter. During the railway strike of 1911 Crowsley had been so much impressed by Tom Mann's article that he cut it out and had several thousand copies printed by the National Labour Press. These he distributed to soldiers in Hyde Park and at Aldershot. He was arrested and charged at Aldershot, and sent for trial. Josiah bailed him out, and, as he had been refused suspension pay by his union, organized help for him during the next weeks. Meanwhile he asked questions in the House and briefed a famous K.C. to defend him. But Crowsley got four months. He is still alive and it is to his kindness that I owe many of the particulars of his case and the following letter which he received in prison:

House of Commons
1.8.1912

My dear Crowsley,

My wife is out of town in Staffordshire and I have sent your letter on to her and she will write to your mother — I don't remember her address.

You have been much more profitably engaged in prison than we have out, and you will not regret having stuck to your point. The main thing is that the dockers have been beaten and smashed utterly, and I don't think you would have enjoyed witnessing the process. The finest thing about it has been the way the men stuck it out for 10 weeks; they only went back last Tuesday.

We had a demonstration about you in Trafalgar Square and got the usual crowd, the police took down in shorthand all I said about the virtues of the Liberal government.

Also we have had a lovely by-election at Hanley. My friend Outhwaite stood as a Liberal, and we polished off the Labour party and the Tories too. All the Single Tax anarchists turned up with *Progress and Poverty* in their hands and won the election as though it was a religious revival.

Write me at once at Moddershall, Stone, Staffs directly you get home and tell me your plans (if you have any). On your way through London you had better call and see Sanders at the Fabian Society, Clements Inn, Strand, especially if you want any funds of which we have plenty.

The Ilkestone people got let off scot-free by Lord Coleridge on promising not to do it again. You see they were mere socialists and had none of your obstinacy or principles! I hope you won't do it again, but will get peacably to work, when and how I do not know.

You will have to come and see us as soon as I can fix it up, when we can talk everything over.

The attack on freedom of opinion in 1912 caused one of those temporary spasms which fling lovers of liberty of every kind and creed into each others arms. Josiah found himself among the founders of the 'Freedom Defence League' with H. G. Wells, Hilaire Belloc and G. K. Chesterton — a mingling of Right and Left, Roman Catholic and Rationalist that defied analysis. In Josiah's words 'it remained active and united for nearly two months'.

From this time forward Josiah was more often against the Government than on its side. 'The handsome young Liberal-Anarchist,' wrote a commentator, 'attacks his own government in and out of season.' His next major tussle with them came over the Mental Deficiency Bill. What he objected to was the compulsory principle.

The bill was to make it possible for mentally defective children to be placed in homes if necessary without the consent of their parents; under one clause it was also possible to incarcerate prostitutes in the same way. His objections are best summed up in his own words in a letter to Mr. Asquith.

To deal with the admitted evil [he wrote], all that is really necessary is to provide funds to help the voluntary institutions. There are thousands of voluntary applications from parents for vacant places in these homes, applications which cannot be accepted owing to insufficient accommodation. If we can meet this demand we shall have done enough, without legislating for the locking up of children against the wishes of their parents, or for the permanent incarceration of the adult feeble-minded.

At somewhat greater length he elaborated his views in the columns of *The Nation*:

To protect the feeble-minded from harming themselves and from ill-usage of others good voluntary homes may be needed on a wide scale but these homes should be really voluntary — i.e. voluntarily entered and voluntarily quitted — refuges, not prisons. One may safely predict that if such homes are really suited to feeble-mind wants, happy, comfortable homes, not institutes, they will be eagerly entered by the poor neglected creatures for whom they are intended and reluctantly left. But the doors must be open, not closed, or who shall say whether the forcible detention for their own good may not be a cruelty as great as that we are pretending to save them from. It is easy to imprison people and silence them and then say, safe from contradiction, that they like it.

To come to what I believe is really inspiring the support which the Bill is getting from many sincere and earnest persons — the propagation of the race by the feeble-minded. It is easy to pose one's judgment and be swayed merely by pity and horror, if one has no practical experience of this subject. Such feelings are excusable in specialists but will not excuse law-makers.

I will not discuss here the dubious subject of the transmission of mental deficiency. The laws of heredity are too undetermined for one to pin faith to any doctrine, much less to legislate according to it. At this stage of knowledge one may not be unreasonable in thinking that there is less danger to society present and future in the marriage of the feeble-minded than in the tyranny of those experts who would force them to unwilling chastity for the sake of a scientific creed which in ten years may be discredited.

95

I do not believe that we can take short cuts in the matter of social regeneration and deal by wholesale legislation with any class of the community. The final cure of Deficiency, or any other degradation of mind or body, must lie in a new and better society; and since immediate cases cannot wait for such distant times, the evil must be combatted in each separate case by individual self sacrifice and devotion, aided with all that public knowledge and public monies can do, but never by the wholesale sacrifice of human liberty nor by putting the most defenceless section of the community at the mercy of a state bureau inspired by Eugenists and directed by medical experts.

The Bill met with a good deal of opposition from others as well as Josiah, although he was undoubtedly the obstructionist in chief. It was accordingly dropped during the session of 1912, a fact which he noted with satisfaction in his press-cuttings book, adding his favourite tag from Milton: 'till good Josiah drove them thence to hell.'

The victory was temporary. Next session the Bill was back before the House and Josiah fought it every inch of the way, now almost alone because the cause was lost. He obstructed doggedly clause by clause, keeping the House up for two nights until three in the morning. The feat got its share of attention in the Press, and was watched as the second night drew out with some interest as a sporting event. How long could the Honourable Member for Newcastle-under-Lyme go on rising to object without a break for rest or refreshment? He was doing it all, it was pointed out, without even the help of a stiff drink or two. A teetotaller, he obstructed hour after hour on a diet of milk chocolate. It was, of course, wholly in vain: every objection was overruled, every amendment voted down. But on principle he fought the bill to the last syllable.

V

Of those who watched the temperance M.P. munching milk chocolate to keep up his strength as he rose, time and again, as lively as before, when everyone else was exhausted, few if any knew the source of his apparently cheerful strength. He clutched, with the whole of his physical and mental being, at the fight in Parliament to save himself from drowning in the hungry ocean of private sorrow. His wife had left him.

What had induced this clever, passionate woman to march out of his life in the same purposeful way as she had entered it, will never be fully known. Human hearts retain their secrets. The reason she gave sounds like something in Ibsen; to live with a man whom you have ceased to love, she argued, was prostitution. She had ceased to love him; therefore she must leave his house.

It had never been a peaceful marriage. Their domestic vessel had ridden high on a sea of passion, splendidly storm-tossed, at other times blessed by moments of glorious calm. But such marriages may be as happy and as permanent as the duller kind; theirs had lasted twenty years and they had seven children.

For some time he could not even discover where she was or what she meant to do. When he was sure she would not come back he put his second daughter in charge of his house — the eldest was already at Cambridge — and in a touching attempt to make his home beautiful for his children bought some more framed photographs of old masters.

Partly to take his mind off the unforgettable grief he accepted in the winter an invitation to visit America and preach the Single Tax from Boston to Chicago.

It was his first visit, but he went inspired by Ralph's stories of a walking tour in the footsteps of Stonewall Jackson, and saturated with knowledge of the War of Independence and the Civil War. Admiration for America was part of the tradition, handed down from 'old Josiah' who in 1778 had 'blessed his stars' that America was free 'as one refuge from the iron hand of tyranny', a sentiment not unique in England during the American War of Independence.

Lecturing to enthusiastic audiences, the disciples of Henry George, and the Georgeite clubs up and down the country, he could almost forget his personal despair. Here the cause was alive, even spreading; the people fresh, vital, enthusiastic, their whole history a monument to the liberties in which he believed.

I gave them the milk of the gospel [he wrote to his second son], and they gave me an ovation. I spoke at Boston, Philadelphia, Washington, Cleveland, Ohio, Chicago and New York several times. The meetings at Philadelphia and at the Coopers Union at New York were perhaps the best. It was at Coopers Union that Henry George used to speak. The whole audience, I should think, came and shook my hand. What really pleased them was that I preached freedom and not taxation, and that I appealed to labour instead of to the politicians . . . I have made hosts of friends.

By the early summer of 1914 he was back in England, then hot with disputes over the Irish question. He fetched three of his children from boarding school on August 1st for a bicycling tour home. The troops they met on the roads made him suddenly doubtful. Yet he was certain there would not be a war; the German Social-Democrats would never support it. But he left the children to go on alone and took the train to London. At a deserted Athenaeum the porter could not change his cheque. 'Sorry sir, the bishops have cleared me out.'

He spoke second after Lord Grey's famous and terrible speech on Monday, August 3rd, 'Honourable Members have not conceived what is going to happen,' he said, 'you are destroying a civilization.' He was convinced with the righteous idealism of the true Liberal that this war was wrong; even the betrayal of the young popular cause by the German Social-Democrats did not shake him.

Two days later, however, he supported the vote of credit in a speech in which he drew the distinction, then not so common as it has since become, between the two Germanies, 'the genial German people' and the military caste. He had been brought up in Germany and to the end of his life he never forgot the good impressions (as well as the bad) that he had received there.

For the first fortnight his opinions swayed dizzily. He was trying to organize, with George Lansbury, a land cultivation committee to stave off the expected famine. He was in touch with Jean Grave, the French anarchist leader, for a united working-class agitation for a just and speedy settlement. He was reading Kinglake's *Crimean War* aloud to the children. Very soon he was writing to a pacifist friend, 'Though a pacifist, I feel now glad that we did not leave France in the lurch, and I would rather fight on than leave the Kaiser triumphant. That, I suppose, is why I should be prepared to fight myself, though you know what I feel about war and killing.' Rapidly his opinions crystallized. 'Namur has fallen,' he wrote to the same friend, 'I do not think it right to *compel* people to go and face it by Act of Parliament unless I go myself.'

His old friend Walter Runciman offered him a job in the Commercial Intelligence Department to help in the plans for diverting German trade, but already he had other ideas. His training as a naval architect and his Boer war experience might both come in useful. If he was still far from enthusiastic for the war itself, he was determined to play an active part. He sought out Churchill at the Admiralty and, in September, after a fortnight's hurried training, landed at Dunkirk in charge of six armoured cars with a machine gun on each.

Before he left he published in the pages of the *Staffordshire Evening Sentinel* a letter explaining to his constituents his reasons for the step he was taking.

> In a few days [he wrote], I shall be leaving for active service in France. This is only what many thousand volunteers from North Staffordshire have done already, or soon will be doing, but, as I have not had an opportunity of speaking here since the war started, I want to use your columns to tell my friends and constituents what it is that compels me to go. Liberals, like myself, love liberty. It is a passion: I cannot explain it. 'You cannot argue with the choice of a soul.' My political work has all been directed to the securing of economic liberty for the worker. I must now leave that struggle to others and to my children. There is other more elementary and more painful work to be done for liberty. It has to be done. All who think like me ought to take part.

CHAPTER V

THE FIRST WORLD WAR

FOR the first two or three days the armoured cars operated from Lille. It was exciting if ineffective; the country was deserted of civilians, but the Uhlan cavalry hopped into the hedges as the little cars came snorting down on them. Nobody then realized how completely the internal combustion engine was going to revolutionize war, but Josiah was getting some idea of what it might do against cavalry, given time and an unlimited supply of cars.

He had little idea of what was happening anywhere else. The second night, coming back to Lille, he found Germans in the suburbs, but broke through only to be told to evacuate quickly. He was next in operation at Berlaar on the Scheldt where the Belgians in vain tried to hold the German advance. The cars were used for reconnoitring — perhaps the first recorded mechanized cavalry. Involved in the retreat — rapidly becoming a rout — of the Belgian infantry, Josiah stopped his car and brewed himself tea in the midst of the fugitives, by way of restoring morale. After two days and nights non-stop evacuation of stores from Ghent to Eccloo, he was asked to abandon his beloved cars and take a load of trucks up the railway to supply the Naval Brigade with petrol and rations at Selzaete on the retreat from Antwerp. Manned by a driver and a guard (who said he could also work the points if necessary) the train lumbered off into the autumn evening through deserted stations, Josiah on the footplate, revolver in hand. Night had fallen before they slowed up for the, at first unrecognizable, obstruction which straggled darkly all across the level crossing at Sas-van-Ghent.

Today there is no need to describe such scenes; in 1914 they were something unimagined except by Mr. H. G. Wells. Standing on his footplate and watching the close packed huddle, 'silent save for the sludge of shuffling feet', pass unendingly by, soldiers and civilians, carts and bicycles and cars, he remembered the *War of the Worlds* and shuddered. They tossed the rations from the trucks to the Belgian troops; the Naval Brigade had long since gone by.

Two days later he sailed for England on a boat crammed with wailing, hopeless, homeless people. In the wind and darkness he went round cheering them in his comprehensible but idiosyncratic French. Touched by the plight of three apparently unprotected and tearful girls he gave them the address of Mrs. Walter Runciman. She was pardonably annoyed when three highly professional and predatory Belgian prostitutes turned up on her doorstep with an introduction from Commander Wedgwood.

II

Some months of training with a new batch of cars followed; then little by little the Gallipoli project unfolded. He was immensely excited. Just before he sailed he wrote to his children: 'I love you all very much, but am much better fitted to be a dashing bandit than the responsible parent of seven.' Perhaps it was the best kind of farewell to have from a father setting out to one of the grimmest theatres of war. Still in command of armoured cars forming part of the Naval Brigade, he sailed from Plymouth at the end of March 1915. The destination, perilous though it might be, was full of wonder and romance to him. He wrote to his mother:

> We have had a lovely yachting trip down the Mediterranean and up through the Aegean islands right here to the plains of Troy which gaze at us across the sunlit waters. Do you remember how you used to read to me of all these islands? It made them seem like home. Salamis and Naxos, Euboea and Lemnos. Here Iphgenia was sacrificed; here Bacchus found Ariadne. The tyrant of the Chersonese reigned just over there . . . Landing anywhere is a little difficult.

Landing was indeed the problem. Josiah was one of those charged with preparing the wreck ship *River Clyde* from which the famous landing on 'V' beach was to be made. The story of those April days in 1915 has been told often and well. I shall quote only from three of his letters. On April 22nd he wrote to his second son (his elder son Charles was with him):

My dear son,

I am writing from my wreck ship — the latest addition to the Navy whose whole existence as such will last but a week. Soon we push off for Tenedos. There we embark 2500 men of the 29th Division Munster and Dublin Fusiliers and Hampshires. Then on Saturday night we move off to within 1½ miles of the shore. At dawn we pile ourselves up on the beach, while the whole fleet shoot over our heads to keep down the Turkish fire.

Once well aground a lighter is fixed at our bows and a steam hopper ahead of that. The men rush out of big ports in the ship's sides and along balconies on to the lighter and hopper and over a brow, dry shod on to the shore. Thereafter our good ship (or what is left of her), forms a landing jetty for the guns and stores.

I have got 18 of my motor cycles and, with them and

the guns, I mean to carry on till I can land my cars in a country where they can move.

My guns are now all in armoured and sandbagged casemates along the decks of the ships; and the men as happy as princes at the chances of a hot fight.

The whole thing is the idea of Commander Unwin, who captains this ship, and calls it the second Wooden Horse of Troy.

You will know long before you get this if I have got through all right. Remember that in the worst case I expect you to look after your three youngest sisters and to get into the House of Commons as soon as possible. . . .

To Winston Churchill he wrote two days later:

H.M.S. *River Clyde*
April 24th, 1915

Dear Churchill,

This ought to be a most interesting letter if it is ever finished, for we are on the wreck ship.

As usual I have fallen in pleasant places. Seeing that the cars were not likely to be of use here for some time, I trained my squadron for working the maxims on their flat feet.

As soon as Hamilton arrived I reported to him (as provided in my blessed Sailing Orders) and soon got fixed up to arm this ship, commanded by Commander Unwin the inventor of the wreck ship idea. We made casemates for our guns, and have also got motor cycles aboard so that we can run our guns (or other people's ammunition) up to Krithia if all goes well. We are attached to the 20th Division under Hunter Weston.

Today, this afternoon, unless the wind again puts us off, 2400 Munsters and Dublins and Hampshires come on board and conceal themselves in the holds of the Wooden Horse. (We are in sight of the windy plains of Troy.) In the ship's side great ports are cut. As soon as the crash comes and we grind ashore, these dragon's teeth spring armed from the ports and race along the balcony to the stem of the vessel; there they pass forward along a steam hopper and thence a drawbridge to dry land.

You may ask why we have not got dozens of wreck ships instead of only one. The answer is that it is an experiment, and only a First Lord makes experiments on a lordly scale, but you can imagine *our* joy at being on the experiment. Of course we may get sunk going in, but bar that, it seems to me the least risky way of landing troops, and you get a serviceable jetty for landing alongside, for other guns and stores.

I must finish this for the first instalment. So six of your maxims rush the heights ¾ mile inland with the troops; then the bikes come to Sedul Bahr and prepare, while I report to the General for further orders. This is better than heckling McKenna.

Three days later he added a second instalment:

Sedd el Bahr
April 27th

We ran ashore on 'V' beach at 6.30, being shelled on the way by 6-in. guns from the Asiatic side. The hopper ran aground on the wrong place. The fire from the shore was heavy, and the original plan could not be worked to. Five tows of five boats each, with some 30 or 40 men in each came on to 'V' beach simultaneously with ourselves, and in ten minutes there were some 400 dead and wounded on the beach and in the water. Not more than 10 per cent. got safe to land and took shelter under the edge of the sand. Some of the Munster Fusiliers tried to land from the *River Clyde* about 7 a.m. after some sort of connection had been made with a spit of rock. Very few of them got safely to land, and General Napier and his Brigade Major were killed on the lighter. Thereafter the wounded cried out all day and for 36 hours — in every boat, lighter, hopper, and along the shore. It was horrible, and all within 200 yards of our guns trying to find and shoot the shooters.

If the *River Clyde* had not been on that beach with 11 maxims on board, not one of the 400 still living on the shore could have survived.

That night we landed the rest of the Munsters and the Hampshires (some 1000 in all). The losses then were small. For three hours I stood on the end of the spit of what had been rock in two foot of water helping the heavily laden men to jump ashore on to submerged dead bodies, and trying to persuade the wounded over whom they had to walk that we should soon get them aboard. This is what went on monotonously: 'Give me your rifle, and your shovel'; 'your left hand'; 'jump wide'; 'it's all right only the kits'; 'keep clear of that man's legs can't you'. And all the time the gangway along one boat worked to and fro on wounded men; and wounded men were brought to the end of the spit and could not get aboard because the other stream was more important and never ending; and there they slowly sank and died.

There was hard fighting all that night ashore; our ship was riddled and we could see nothing and not help. But the casualties then were small. So far we had little help from the fleet, but on Monday morning, all our men (say 3000 reduced to 2000) being ashore, the *Queen Elizabeth* and others, made the semi-circle of hills and village and fort, a lyddite ruin, and our Munsters, Dublins and Hampshires helped on the left by some who had landed at 'W' beach, won the hills. So we now hold 1 mile from the beach, all round the village castle and crest. I have just come down from the picket line where we have been standing to arms and shooting all night long — my third sleepless night. The French have landed 3000 and relieved us.

Our guns and men have won golden opinions from the military. Apparently we covered their attack very well yesterday, besides saving them on Sunday.

And now let me tell you of the deeds of heroism I witnessed. It is pleasanter and I would not have believed them possible.

Midshipman Drury of the *Clyde* swam to the hopper,

was wounded in the head, got a line off the hopper and got somehow back to the ship with it. Commander Unwin, maddened by the failure of his landing plan, stood up alone on the hopper and hauled, surrounded by dead and wounded. He was slightly wounded. He went in again and rowed to the wounded on the rock jetty and loaded them into the boat under fire.

One of our men, J. H. Russell, seeing him wounded and unable to lift the men out of the water, went overboard, and swam to him. He was shot through the stomach and with Unwin lay in the water as though dead for a while, got somehow into the boat in a lull, and were pulled back to the ship by a line.

The wounded were still crying and drowning on that awful spit. Lieut. Tidsdale RND took a boat, one of the *Clyde's* sailors and one of my men, Rumming. They got four men aboard before Tidsdale and the sailor were shot and wounded. Hiding behind the side of the boat they walked and swam it back. I saw one of the wounded stretch out his hand and stroke Rumming's as he hung on to the side, the most pathetic thing I have ever seen. Rumming volunteered again to go ashore with me in the dark, and stood (on the dead), for another 3 hours on that horrible spit under occasional fire. I have officially recommended him and J. H. Russell for the V.C., but I do not know *who* ought really to do that or what course such a recommendation takes.

In the evening my Sub-Lieut. Parkes, C.P.O. John Little and P.O.s Barton, Tailyour, Cecil Murray, went out to help detachments of wounded on the beach. They went westward to the furthest boat's crew, about a mile, landed two wounded from one sinking boat, found in the furthest boat 7 wounded, 9 dead (the shells will keep going over my head and bursting 50 yards further, and I have to stop at the end of each pair of lines and lie down. I will indicate by an × in future) and two maxims, and that boat they rowed back to the ship × the Turks were not shooting, but they passed them within 50 yards like cats in × the dark.

Then × yesterday the Munsters, without officers, could not face the last bit of the charge on the old castle hill. They were dead tired, not afraid. Col. Wylie, Intelligence Officer, being on board the *Clyde* ran ashore and without cap or rifle × dashed up to them and led them on, and fell at the crest.

Just 100 yards from me by the beach lie, each two yards from the other, facing the enemy, 5 heroic Munsters. Right at the beginning on Sunday, after four-fifths of their comrades had fallen these five ran forward to cut the wire entanglements, a hopeless thing to attempt, but what courage it must have required.

You may be very well satisfied with your 3rd Squadron of 'armoured cars'. As soon as they and we are rested we are going forward on foot, with the 29th Division.

I am going to lie down and sleep, the first sleep for three eternal days and nights.[1]

On May 1st, after that fearful landing, came the Turkish attack. In the counter-attack on May 6th Josiah was wounded. He described it later:

We were to attack at dawn. There was no artillery preparation, no enemy to be seen, no objective set that I ever heard of. We just went forward. Five hundred yards on we dug the guns into pits, dug hard to get under cover from the shrapnel. I ran from gun to gun, a hen with too many chickens. Our losses were very heavy; at last I, too, was hit, and went down pole-axed all out in the open. Lieutenant Parkes and another jumped out to help me, but my wound at the top of the left groin was making me feel very sick. Coke was dead, Illingworth was wounded. Parkes must carry on. Also, just before, a man carrying the gun had been wounded and I had not let them carry him in. He could wait and so I waited, wondering if I was bleed-

[1] In his *World Crisis*, vol. II, pp. 319-20, Mr. Churchill writes: 'The whole landing encountered a bloody arrest. The survivors lay prone under the lip of the Beach, and but for the fire of the machine-guns of Commander Wedgwood's armoured car squadron which had been mounted in the bows of the *River Clyde*, would probably have been exterminated.'

ing to death. Then, bullets were chipping the stones beside
me; that gave me a sudden panic and I tried to crawl
back home.

After that the mists of unconsciousness and nightmare came down on him. As he was carried down to
the shore he was inspired by the sympathetic glance of
an Irish friend in the direction of his wound to an
epigram half Rabelais, half House of Commons —
'Thank God my seat is safe'. A tumble of historic and
romantic memories flickered in his pain-darkened
mind. Through the tent-flap Ian Hamilton asked
another casualty how he was, and got the classic
heroic answer, 'All right sir; how's the battle going?'
His mind stumbled after a quotation:

> Men say the earliest word he spoke
> Was 'Friends, how goes the fight?'

Later, seeing a friend looking for him among the
inarticulate, half-unrecognizable wounded, on the
deck of the hospital ship, and thinking he would not
be found, he remembered Edith looking for Harold
among the Saxon dead after Hastings. He was found
by his friend Francis MacLaren who saved his life by
getting him to a surgeon in the nick of time.

Two days later he managed to scrawl in indelible
pencil to his mother:

> Churchill's brother kindly came to see me and said he
> would see that you had news of my safety through Winston
> himself. The Generals have all been most kind and compli-
> mentary. I expect to be fit for anything in the fighting line
> again in a few months and now look upon myself as a com-
> pound of Marbot and Belisarius (or was it Narses). I am
> very proud of being the first Wedgwood to be hit, and also
> very satisfied at having hit back.

THE LAST OF THE RADICALS

At Alexandria an old friend, Maurice Amos, now a judge of the Egyptian courts, turned up to lend him books. He was soon writing cheerfully to his children, saying that he had become 'as skilled at dodging shells as though they were oakapples on the roof of the Ark'. To his son Josiah he added:

> I have seen more slaughter in that fourteen nights than is given to the lot of most men, but as soon as I am well, I am going back, for I would not have missed it for the world. There is something glorious in getting through it, in keeping your men up to the scratch, in seeing them one after another rise to the ranks of heroes, from counter jumpers, and setting an example to regular troops.

From Alexandria he was moved to Malta, where he passed an unhappy convalescence, staring out at the endless sea and a prey to thoughts about his broken home. Someone sent him Chesterton's recently collected poems; this was the kind of poetry he particularly liked and he had friendly recollections of the author ever since their association in the short-lived Freedom Defence League. They fell into correspondence again. Chesterton wrote:

My dear Wedgwood,

> I adopt this prosaic mode of address for fear of being censored, interned, or shot for bringing the King's uniform into contempt by making mistakes about your proper title. But if we were Oriental and could naturally express our admiration by titles, it would be an understatement to call you Brother of the Sun and Moon and Uncle of all the Stars. And if it were possible to correspond entirely in poetry (I wish it was), I should be better able to say what I feel on receiving a letter from so complete a soldier of freedom, both in the Senate and the Field — as they would have said in the XVIII century. I had always admired more than I can say your Parliamentary stand against the plutocrats — the

politicians who do literally, like the Germans, fight with poisoned gas. When it comes to fighting the Germans and Turks in a bodily way as well and being wounded, I find the limits of prose altogether too narrow for me. I only hope you will soon be well enough to give us that first-hand account of the landing on the beach, which deserves to be referred to in better verses than mine. The little book of my stuff was very courageously put together by my wife when I was too ill to do anything; I have hardly dared to look at it: I do not know on what principle minor inclusions or omissions were made, but I am pretty sure it was a good one. However, the War (that much more respectable subject), calls me, though I suppose it sounds horrible to say so, with a sort of satisfaction too enormous to find expression. At last a poor but honest journalist can have the national sentiment without the shadow of an arrière pensée. When my illness was beginning I was bothered about not being able to follow your example. But I am so proud of England now that I should not even care if she were ashamed of me.

III

Back in London by the summer, Josiah received his D.S.O. from the King, spent some of the autumn in the new Ministry of Munitions and went on a week's rapid visit to the Western Front.

An expedition against German possessions in Africa was now projected in which he hoped to be included. But while most of his thoughts were on such matters as these he had time to spare for the cause of conscientious objectors. He disapproved of bullying minorities or compelling men against conscience. His children, brought up to develop and defend their individual opinions, were divided on the issue of conscience; to

one of them, now leaning towards pacifism, he
wrote:

> I do so sympathize with your temptation to become a
> pacifist . . . Why must you and I always jump on to the
> weaker side? That is why I am fighting for France. We
> really must beware of this cult of the minority; it is conceit; it
> is contrariness; I know you *think* it is chivalry.

His two elder daughters were both strong pacifists;
feeling ran high against their point of view but, he
promised, 'I shall come straight to the Ark and rescue
you from the hands of the police or the mob in the
style of a democratic hero in the French Revolution.'
The Ark was already the refuge of C.O.s and stranded
enemy aliens of all kinds.

On November 10th, 1915, when the House debated
the conduct of the war, he spoke at some length, defending those responsible for the Gallipoli expedition
and the men on the spot against the vehement, but
not always informed, attacks of those who had no
first hand experience. 'Even worse examples of
terrible mismanagement,' he pointed out were by no
means unknown in the history of British warfare; he
cited half a dozen from the eighteenth and nineteenth
centuries:

> It is by remembering these things, I think, that you are in
> a better position to criticize the Government than by think-
> ing that everything in the past has always gone well with us
> in wartime, and that in this war there has been exceptional
> blundering. We have always blundered in the past and have
> always pulled through in the end, and the worse blunder
> you get into, the more the credit for getting out of it . . . I
> am one of those who entirely approve of the inception of the
> Dardanelles expedition. I believe at the time it was justified,
> even although it was a gamble. If we had succeeded in

forcing the Dardanelles, the success would have been enormous, and the result to the whole course of the war would have been decisive ... That is what you have got to do in wartime. You have got to take risks. You cannot carry on war on the principle of limited liability or insurance.

He continued to deal, from his personal knowledge, with the various scandals of the campaign, the medical provision, the hospital ships, the disastrous Suvla Bay expedition. While he defended much that had been done, he was emphatic that a different and quicker system of Army promotion was essential and that to restore morale we should adopt the French method of recalling all Generals who failed, whether they were responsible for what had happened or merely unlucky.

General Sir Ian Hamilton wrote to him the following day:

Dear Wedgwood,
    Quite apart from your views, it was a huge relief to me to feel the note of *knowledge* running through your speech in the House when I read it this morning. Thank the Lord someone in that august assemblage really does grasp the difficulties. As to what has passed since I saw you half dead but full of pluck in the clearing station at Helles I'd so much like to have a few words with you. ...

The acquaintance, thus taken up again, developed into a lasting friendship.

In December, however, he went to Africa on the staff of General Smith-Dorrien. 'We left Paddington at midnight,' he told his mother, 'in pitch darkness, amid a host of unknowns who cried good luck and warmly grasped our hands.' On board the ship he met the actress Wish Wynne whose performance as Alice Chalice in Arnold Bennett's *Buried Alive* had given him great delight. He called her 'Mrs. Alice Chalice' and was disappointed to discover in the midst of a promising flirtation that she was Mrs. Somebody-else. For the rest of the journey he urged the passengers to learn Swahili from a group of missionaries on board; but he did not get very far with it himself.

The African campaign brought him into new country which he described with enthusiasm to his mother.

> It is like the garden of Eden, and the beasts are as numerous and as inquisitive as in mediæval Italian paintings. The impala jump bushes eight feet high; the great bearded gnu look at one with impertinent surprise, the zebras frolic and swish their tails.

But Smith-Dorrien had died on the way out and at first the campaign did not go well. Pushing in as always without authority or invitation, Josiah had gone to Pretoria on his way up from the Cape and seen General Smuts. The situation, he said with his usual forthrightness, was not happy. The Germans had already defeated the British troops in East Africa. The present expedition had lost General Smith-Dorrien by sickness on the voyage. Would he, Smuts, accept the East African command and bring up a South African force? The same offer was in fact made by the British Government a little later and accepted with results that belong to history.

But Josiah was the kind of man Smuts liked. They came of comparable puritan stock and believed in the same things. Besides, Josiah loved, and was loved by the Boers. An old 'bitter-ender' of Ermelo days, now a Colonel of the 3rd South African Horse, leapt off his horse at meeting and flung his arms round his neck.

He was not, however, to be long in Africa: just long

enough to write a letter to his mother in triumph from a taken German camp 'sitting at a German table, using a German pen'. Smuts' lightning cavalry went forward too fast for the machine guns and cars in that wild country. So he came back to England and to the war in Parliament.

While he was in Africa the 1916 Easter Rising had taken place in Ireland. Roger Casement, who had been landed from a German submarine on April 21st, was arrested on the 24th and sent to London. Josiah had always had sympathy with aspirations for Irish independence and furthermore he had been on terms of personal friendship with Roger Casement who had helped him with sympathy and a subscription when he was fighting for Tom Mann and Fred Crowsley. Josiah knew that nothing could be done for Casement now, but the personal letter which he wrote to Redmond reflects what was felt at the time by many of his friends:

Dear Redmond,
    I hardly know whether, for Casement's own sake, he had not better be shot, but I don't like the shooting of him. You on the spot will of course know what best to do, but if you are thinking of trying to get a commutation (and if there is still time), a letter from me may help your hand.
    Casement was a friend of mine, and I have still a great admiration for his wonderful unselfishness and generous enthusiasms. We ought not to have his blood on our heads, when the cause for which we are fighting is as near as we believe it to be the cause of God.
    We both know that he is mad — mad with that glorious madness that sees only the heavens and cares nothing for this earth. There is nothing mean and self-seeking about that form of lunacy, and for it one can only have the deepest pity and charity.

The letter was written on May 9th, 1916; Casement was tried for high treason in June and, after his appeal had been dismissed, hanged at Pentonville, early in August.

That summer Josiah returned to London. The Somme offensive had begun with casualties vaster than any known to the recorded history of war. 1916-1917 was a year of disaster. It was also, as such years will be, a year of feverish gaiety. To all intents a bachelor, in the prime of life, attractive and a war-hero, Josiah now invaded new reaches of society: the Army and the landed aristocracy at the hospitable table of Sir Ian Hamilton; diplomacy and the arts with Lady Cunard. In a burst of enthusiasm she asked him to bring his family to her box at the opera. Dressing for the opera was rarely included in the education of the Wedgwood family: 'Five of them turned up dressed like nothing on earth,' he records, and Lady Cunard's composure was all but unequal to the occasion. He followed literature with a new friend, the novelist Dorothy Richardson, and became a temporary devotee at one and the same time of the stage and of Lilian Braithwaite. He was a member of Churchill's famous 'Other Club', which met once a fortnight for dinner at the Savoy. One minor casualty of the war had been his temperance principles.

In August he had been appointed to the Royal Commission on Mesopotamia. The gradual unrolling of the evidence of confusion and mismanagement in the Mesopotamian campaign made a sinister accompaniment to the current news from Europe. The Viceroy of India and his chief of staff were the object of bitter criticism but the Commission did not feel that 'the evidence before us justifies attaching to Lord Hardinge (the Viceroy) and Sir Beauchamp Duff alone the blame for the mistakes and shortcomings connected with the Mesopotamia expedition'.

Josiah thought differently and appended a minority report, differing 'rather in emphasis than in substance'. The difference lay in his placing the chief blame squarely on the principals rather than apportioning it among many in positions of less authority, whose chief fault had been that they estimated the chances of victory rather too sanguinely.

'Censure for honest human error,' wrote Josiah, 'has nothing in common with the censure we should pass on an attitude of unwillingness to help in war. If we confound mistakes with crimes the result is a dangerous leniency towards crime.' After summing up parts of the evidence which he thought significant, Josiah ended:

I cannot resist the conclusion that the above evidence points to a want of willingness to help on the part of the Indian Government — that is on the part of Lord Hardinge and Sir Beauchamp Duff. That this unwillingness affected adversely the expedition to Mesopotamia is obvious. Had they thrown themselves heart and soul into getting India to do all that was humanly possible both in men and material, the whole course of the war might have been altered . . . It would appear that, in fact, the Army Administration in India was jealous of the Army at home; they wished to retain the magnitude of their command; they felt they were neglected, 'out of the picture', and they determined, perhaps unconsciously, to be obstructive. It will be unfortunate if an attitude of this sort is passed over.

From these conclusions he passed to one last recommendation 'that we should no longer deny to Indians "the full privileges of citizenship", but should allow them a large share in the government of their own country and in the control of that Bureaucracy which in this war, uncontrolled by public opinion, has failed to rise to British standards. Lord Kitchener said it would be better to lose India than to lose that for which we are fighting the war — the glorious traditions of a people old in liberty'.

He had thought a good deal about Indian freedom before the war, but it was his experience on the Mesopotamia Commission which turned him from a mere sympathizer to an eloquent partisan of self-government.

The sequel was a minor incident in the House when Mr. Ronald McNeill tabled a Motion condemning the Minority report in offensive terms as 'intemperate'. In the ensuing debate he failed to support his motion, which rather surprised the Speaker who had arranged to call Josiah to answer him, and exasperated Josiah who had counted on defending himself and his report against the motion of condemnation.

It was, to say the least of it, Parliamentary ill-manners to table a provocative motion and then give its object no opportunity of replying. Josiah later in the debate called on McNeill to do so, but he slid out with: 'If I can give satisfaction to the honourable and gallant gentleman on any other occasion I am perfectly willing to do so.'

The phrase was not very happily chosen; Josiah responded by sending round a letter asking for satisfaction in the good old eighteenth-century fashion if Mr. McNeill would appoint a place to meet him with pistols. Mr. McNeill preferred to offer a rather sheepish personal explanation in the House, and the matter dropped.

It is worth recording because it was characteristic of Josiah to believe in the duel. It matched his belief in individual responsibility and personal courage. He had some years before attempted to challenge a man on a personal quarrel, and he was widely believed, at a later time, to have challenged General Dyer after the Amritsar massacre. No one ever accepted these challenges, but they were made in perfect good faith and he was, I believe, disappointed that he never had the chance of carrying out this interesting historic rite. It appealed to all that was romantic in his nature, and he liked the defence of justice and his principles to have a romantic as well as a progressive air.

Among the letters he received at this time there is one which was evidently treasured. It was from that fine soldier whom he so much admired, Sir Ian Hamilton:

Dear Wedgwood,

I have just read a summary of your Minority Report in yesterday's *Morning Post* and I cannot resist sending you a line to tell you of the relief I experienced in doing so and in finding an understanding point of view. I am glad you did not join in the condemnation of the quality of optimism in war or in the desire to down those who in war have a try.

Words like these far outweighed with him the waspish criticisms of lighter men.

v

It had become very clear that without American intervention the war would drag on interminably.

In the autumn of 1916 Josiah went over to Washington on an unofficial mission. He met, not Wilson with whom he would probably have had little sympathy, but Colonel House whom he at once entirely understood. What he had with him was an extraordinary document which he had drawn up in collaboration with his friend the unrepentent idealist Noel-Buxton, for a proposed European peace. It included among other idealistic terms the internationalization of the African colonies, the protection of Suez, Tangier and Palestine by the United States and the solution of the Alsace-Lorraine problem by joining it to Switzerland. What part this document played, if any, in the diplomacy of the war it is hard to tell. At the time Colonel House was interested, kept it for reference, and failed to return it.

Josiah, meanwhile, toured the beloved country, meeting old friends, making new ones, speaking everywhere, explaining the war, its causes, its aims, and the democratic principles involved. But American isolationism was strong and he was not hopeful when he left.

In *The Times*, the *Chronicle* and the *Daily News* he advertised the virtues of President Wilson, propaganda which might be helpful; he could not know. The intervention of America, desperately needed, still hung in the balance. One April day a card was brought in to him in the House and he went out to find a friend from the American Embassy. 'I came to let you know,' he said, 'we shall be coming in tonight.' Colonel House, coming over three months later told him, 'Your visit to America was the most useful we have had in this war.' It was impossible, of course, to know exactly what he meant by that. But gratifying.

In the autumn of 1917 the long-drawn tragedy of Passchendaele ran its course. Josiah, with information and imagination, was, with many another, appalled at the mounting casualties and the vision ever present to the mind's eye. In secret session in December he placed before the House his own account of the casualties in the mud. As he left Mr. Bonar Law came after him: 'Wedgwood,' he said, 'you did right to say what you did. But never let any of that be known outside. The public could not bear it.'

A week later, in open session, he repeated the substance of his speech but without the more dreadful details. 'I was by the side of a soldier on a bus the other day,' he said, 'and I noticed on his shoulder the almost sacred word *Gallipoli*. I asked him how long he had been back. He replied, "Two days." I said, "Were you in the last business?" He did not turn towards me at all, but looked straight in front of him and replied, "Unfortunately I was at Passchendaele." I did not know quite what to say, but I asked, "Does it haunt you?" and he turned round towards me exactly as a child would do, and said, "It will haunt me for the rest of my life." I said nothing else. Anyone who has seen the casualty list or anyone who understands what to read into those casualty lists, will see what Passchendaele has meant.'

The March Revolution in Russia broke like the sound of trumpets on the ears of the Radicals and the Left. A free Parliamentary Russia and the end of the proverbial tyranny of the Czar; this was the dawn they had hoped for, and they welcomed it with jubilation in the Albert Hall. It was, of course, the constitutional government of Kerensky, not the Red Dawn. When that was superseded in October, Josiah was sent by a bewildered War Office, urged on by the *Daily News*, to see if he could locate the remnant of the Kerensky government, believed to be functioning at Tomsk.

Churchill gave him characteristic advice at parting. 'Simply get in a locomotive,' he said, 'and push as far into Russia as you can.' Josiah was delighted with the prospect. 'Picture me wrapped in sheepskins, driving a loco,' he wrote to Ralph, 'or pretending to be a dissolute journalist or amiably waving an unloaded pistol and talking bad Bosch or worse Russky.'

On this occasion, when asked what rank he wished to assume on the British Army's business, he said, 'What about Colonel?' Rather to his surprise his interlocutor breathed a sigh of relief: 'Thank Heaven. I thought you might stand out for General.' So Colonel Wedgwood he became, and remained for the next twenty-five years, to the annoyance of Colonel Blimp.

He crossed the Atlantic, crossed a war-conscious active America, crossed the Pacific, bathing on the sands of Honolulu by the way, landed at last at Tokyo. 'Here's to the Great Adventure,' he wrote to his son, 'I shall never grow old.' He pushed on into Mukden through a chaos of conflicting allegiances, came at last to Harbin where the Chinese, Japanese and two sorts of Russian government all claimed mastery — 'an anarchy under three consuls and a railway guard', he described it. Here he learnt that whatever government there had ever been at Tomsk had been liquidated. He cabled home, and was told to make Vladivostok and report on the situation. 'Fear of our ally (Japan) was written up large over Eastern Asia,' he noticed with an insight which was prophetic.

On the way to Vladivostok, Bolshevik troops boarded the train 'clothed like wild animals in furs and dirt'. Not quite sure what they wanted he took out his revolver, sat on it and awaited events. Nothing happened. After a little time he ventured forth and found one of them mounting guard in the corridor. 'What are you doing here?' he asked. 'To protect the English officer,' he was told. The rest of the troops were searching the train for smuggled vodka; Josiah watched with unconcealed respect as they solemnly smashed every bottle they found. A friendly offer of cigarettes which he made to some of the men was refused with equally austere self-discipline.

He rather enjoyed Vladivostok, where the band in the restaurant struck up 'Tipperary' whenever he appeared, apparently under the impression that it was a non-monarchical version of the National Anthem. But there was nothing more that could profitably be done in Russia. He cabled home to the War Office that their stores should be retrieved, for it would be criminal folly to finance or to supply the counter-revolution as things now stood. The War Office, which had not sent him to give them this kind of advice, instantly recalled him.

Before he left Vladivostok he had heard on a naval wireless the news of the March push. The Germans had reached Amiens. He got back to London to learn that his elder son was missing. It was a painful summer; made more painful by his decision to go ahead with his divorce and give Ethel the statutory causes 'desertion and adultery' which were at that time essential to procure it. Desertion came first and the relevant columns of the press contained in May 1918 the statement that Josiah Clement Wedgwood had abandoned his wife and seven children. To anyone knowing the facts the statement was grotesque. Several of his children were still living with him at the Ark. But the facts were not generally known, and the afternoon after the announcement the atmosphere of the House was, for the first and only time in his life, icily hostile.

It was in July that he dined at Ian Hamilton's with Hilaire Belloc; they got on to their favourite topic of military history, and went home together to Belloc's flat. From the battles of the past, they came to the battles of the present. Belloc traced the lines outside Soissons with beer on the table-top. 'This now, this hour, is the turning point,' said Belloc, and proved to be right.

For Josiah, as for so many others, the November Armistice seemed the opening of a new world, the world made safe for democracy.

CHAPTER VI

THE 'TWENTIES

THE war had been won, but Josiah was one of the anxious minority who did not care for the temper of militant reaction and bitterness that simultaneous European revolutions and allied victories had created among the winners. Staunch to his ideals of a new world, he strongly supported President Wilson's fourteen points and the idea of the League of Nations. His sympathies were at least partly with the agitation for Home Rule in Ireland and altogether with the movement for Indian independence. The victory over German imperialism could not, he felt, be better marked than by the granting of self-government to India. He had not in the war years forgotten the doctrines of Henry George, but his attempt to introduce a Land Value Assessment Rating Bill at about this time was defeated.

His devotion to the service of the forgotten or oppressed had been intensified rather than diminished by the experiences of the war. On a visit to Belgium a few weeks after the armistice, he was immediately perturbed by the conditions of the German prisoners of war working there. 'They look starved and cold, and their huts made of old corrugated pieces of iron are even worse. I don't like slavery,' he wrote in a letter home, and resolved to raise the question in the House of Commons. There, too, he asked repeated questions about the treatment of aliens and pacifists, and campaigned for the release of conscientious objectors, many of whom were still in prison six months after the end of the war. His interest in the oppressed did not, however, begin or end with those who were already in opposition to society. He was also concerned with better conditions for post office workers and the protection of probationer nurses who, as he bluntly remarked in a debate on the Nurses Registration Bill, 'are notoriously bullied by matrons'.

He had by now almost wholly parted company with the Liberals and it was as an Independent Radical that he presented himself for re-election to the people of Newcastle-under-Lyme in December 1918.

> I come before you [he wrote in his election address], the same impenitent Independent Radical that you first elected in 1906; older and wiser perhaps, possibly with less confidence of success — I hope with fewer enemies — but with the same ideals and with an even better proved determination to fight against injustice to the end.

He was unopposed as the Government gave him 'the coupon' out of a general feeling of goodwill for his services in the war, although he had not asked for it.

In spite of his championship of unpopular minorities, no one could deny his distinguished war record. He was very willing to use the reputation acquired in the firing line to protect from misrepresentation the moral courage of those whose consciences had kept them out of it. Yet there were militarists in Newcastle who objected when they heard that he had been speaking in Blackburn for the pacifist Philip Snowden.

The storm broke over a more private matter. A few days after he had been returned unopposed, his wife was granted her decree nisi on grounds of desertion and adultery. On the following Sunday the vicar of a Newcastle parish, the Reverend Mr. Sinker, denounced him from the pulpit at the morning, afternoon and evening services, and called on the congregation to sign a petition against him. The wording of the protest is so strange a social document as to deserve quotation. Mr. Sinker reminded his parishioners of their husbands, brothers and sons, killed in the war:

They died, they gave their all, that England might live, that she might emerge from all the horror and misery of war a nobler England still than she has ever been. Are we to wrong them now? Our own dead, men of Newcastle, men of Wolstanton, Chesterton, Silverdale, and all those gallant villages that stand with us — are they to look down and behold us content to leave Newcastle to speak in the great Council of the Nation through the voice of an adulterer?

The protest evoked a fairly large response of the same self-righteous kind, and several women wrote to the Press in terms such as these:

Sir,
        I should like to thank the Vicar, Mr. Sinker, for his outspoken remarks about the member for Newcastle. It is quite time we all tried to do something to make the world better and cleaner for the dear boys who have suffered so much for us.
                                        A Mother of the Boys.

Another writer supported the Vicar's 'fearless protest'. She, too, objected to 'being represented in Parliament by an adulterer. John the Baptist sealed such a protest with his life . . . We women feel burning indignation . . . Can we trust such a man with the making of our laws for purity?'
Voices no less emphatic were, however, raised on the other side. 'One of the Congregation' wrote to the papers vehemently protesting against the 'misuse of

God's House on Sunday last'. Ten ministers of religion
in the constituency signed Mr. Sinker's protest, but at
least as many boldly defended the black sheep. Among
these was the staunch vicar of the other large Newcastle parish. They took their stand on the biblical
principle, 'Judge not that ye be not judged'. Being
aware of the peculiar state of the divorce law, they
were ready to believe that their member might not be
so guilty as he had chosen to let himself appear.

Josiah, of course, could say nothing. The decree was
not yet absolute. Moreover, he had battles on at Westminster as well. He had fought, like many others, for
a better world. In the early months of 1919 he saw his
hopes of that world destroyed by popular passion, fear
and hatred. He had always believed in 'two Germanies'; he saw that at Versailles the new Republican
Germany was being starved and stunted from birth.
He had always believed in the rights of the people, in
revolutions bloody but glorious, by which ancient
privilege, rank and wealth and bureaucracy, should
be overthrown. Such revolutions he saw, or thought
he saw, in Russia and Hungary. He was too generous
in his hopes of them, but he hated the ill-disguised
mean fears and bitterness of most of those who fought
against them. During the war his fellow men had
seemed fine and noble. Now that it was over his
generous nature recoiled at the prejudice and pettiness
of the worst and at the delusions of the better men who
filled the House of Commons after the Khaki election.
Those were the days of the Red Terror, the recent
murder of·the Tsar, horrifying stories of Spartacist
atrocities in Berlin, and of Bela Kun in Hungary. It
needed a great deal of courage on the part of the small
minority in the House of Commons to raise their
voices against the incoherent babble of prejudice and

rage, to call for some coolness of judgment, some examination of the facts, to protest against the making of peace, or the further making of war, in an atmosphere of hysterical hatred, or fear, or triumph, or lies.

While in Staffordshire he opened the papers to find his constituents protesting at his morals, in London his post contained anonymous threats. 'Vengeance is mine!' proclaimed an ill-written postcard. 'The mills of God, etc. From an Englishman to a Bolsh.' One of the Colonel Blimps of the day sent him another: 'Colonel Wedgwood, you shame the English army. How much did you obtain for this propaganda?'

In April he broke finally with the Liberals and joined the I.L.P. A week or two later he received an unexpected letter, the first he had had for a long time, and the last, as far as I know, that he ever received from that quarter. Ethel wrote:

Dear Josiah,
King's Proctor notwithstanding I want to congratulate you on the fight you are putting up and also on your liberation from the Liberals whose interest in the fate of Europe seems to be strictly subordinate to Party requirements. You must be having a good deal of trouble with the constituents. Never mind them. Fight it out!

Between the unrest in India, the revolutions in Eastern Europe, the Peace Treaty and his private troubles, the first six months of 1919 were a restless time. He protested (not alone) vehemently and vainly against the punitive bombing of Indian villages, the abominable policy initiated at that time to quell the rising tide of Indian nationalism. Indian soldiers had fought in the war on promises of independence for their country. Those promises, as they saw it, were not being honoured. There were other causes of unrest beside the ferment of ideas — liberal from England and Marxist from Russia — which now made up a devil's brew of confusion in the sub-continent. There was grave economic trouble. There was the profound and genuine re-awakening of Indian life and thought. There was the ancient bitterness between Hindu and Moslem. A problem so huge and complex defies brief analysis, and things were not so simple as Josiah sometimes thought. But it was his habit to cut the Gordian knot of political dilemma with the sword-stroke of a single question: is it Just?

He welcomed the India Reform Bill, but judged it inadequate by the standard of India's deserts and the hopes that had been raised. He disapproved of the communal franchise and the property qualification for the franchise. When unrest increased and the Rowlatt Act was passed to stamp it out his voice was raised in angry protest. His chief objection was that the Act, giving powers of arbitrary arrest, had been passed without the consent of the Indian members of the Viceroy's Legislative Council.

In the first place, if the Indians — not by a majority, but by absolute unanimity — on the Viceroy's Legislative Council say that they do not want that Act, then that measure ought not to be passed into law. Conceive what it would be here if you had legislation not by a minority, but legislation against the unanimous wish of this House... I do not suppose there is one man in 100,000 in India who knows what the Rowlatt Act is, but they do know that their elected representatives voted against it to a man, and that in spite of that it was forced on the country. That, I believe, is the principle reason of the late riots — this absolute disregard of all those British traditions which are always upon our lips, but which we do not always conform to when it comes to dealing with people whom we have governed for their good for so long. The fact that you are legislating against the unanimous wish of the people, whether it be good or bad legislation, is bound to damn that legislation and to give it no possible chance of operating with success. This Rowlatt Act is the most lawless law, to use the word of Mr. Bannerjee in the India Parliament, ever passed into law.

Meanwhile the Versailles Treaty was signed. He saw it, to use the words of another statesman of another treaty, as *une semence éternelle de guerres*. It had done none, or very few, of the things for which he hoped. He saw the possibility of a new and different Germany destroyed at the outset by terms which undermined both the *morale* and the economic basis of the Weimar Republic. When Lloyd George entered the House of Commons after concluding the treaty, almost the whole of the assembly rose to cheer him. There were perhaps half a dozen, of whom Josiah was one, who remained seated and silent.

On June 23rd, 1919, Ethel's decree was made absolute. Two days later he married, at Chelsea Registry Office, Florence Willett, an old friend who had been away from England teaching and lecturing in America for the past seven years. He had first got to know her when she was coaching his two elder daughters some years before the war. When she left England to take up work on the further side of the globe she was followed by affectionate letters from all the family, and this epistolary friendship had matured over the years, in Josiah's case to a profound community of ideas and interests. In the autumn of 1914, when his own pacifist views were undergoing their metamorphosis, he had discussed the pacifist dilemma with her in letters across the seas. She herself was at the time a convinced pacifist. On his visit to America their paths crossed once for a matter of a few hours.

This second marriage enabled him to build up again, very quickly, the background of home that was so necessary to him. Florence shared his interests and entered into his political life with all her heart. She shared his compassionate outlook on the unfortunate of all kinds and classes, and believed as profoundly as he did in justice and the brotherhood of man. During twenty-four years of political storm and stress, she gave him support in public and serenity at home. Her own family background had been Puritan to the point of austerity; in him she found that high moral standards and a sense of duty need not exclude laughter. His gaiety was a constant delight which seemed always new to her and their joint pleasure in vintage family jokes and the familiar joys of everyday life was ever renewed.

Immediately the ceremony was over he took his wife for a brief visit to Paris, hardly a honeymoon for they were accompanied by his second daughter. She had become engaged to a Hungarian towards the end of the war. He had been at school with her brothers, and had been cut off in England by the declaration of war when scarcely more than a boy. Thanks to the intervention of Josiah he had spent most of his internment cultivating vegetables round the Ark. The war over he had returned home, and thither (revolution or no) his future wife was now set on following him.

Before leaving Paris Josiah wrote and dispatched a letter to the local paper, the *Staffordshire Evening Sentinel*. From the beginning of the attack on his character he had been determined to justify his conduct as soon as he was free to speak. He owed no less to the constituents who had faithfully supported him.

All his life he remained curiously unprepared for public reaction and when he wrote and posted his letter of explanation he had no idea at all beyond that of satisfying his constituents and answering his local critics. Thus he was far away accompanying his daughter to her future husband in a revolutionary Hungary while his private affairs were making headline news in England. This was the letter he wrote:

Sir,

When I was divorced, the Rector of Newcastle, with great charity, declined to join in the clerical outcry against me. I made up my mind then, that, in justice to him and to those like him, I must, when the time came, write this letter, however unpleasant it is to publish my private affairs for the whole of North Staffordshire.

My married life was a very happy one, until in 1913 my wife ceased to love me. She is one of those who believe that to live with a man you do not love is prostitution, and we separated. For many years I kept hoping that she would change, for after twenty years the break always seems inconceivable. I offered to start again in a new country, where no one would know us. It was all useless, and when I came back from Africa in 1916, and failed again, I at last realized that plans had to be made to reconstruct my life and home.

I consulted a colleague, a leading K.C. in the House. He told me that there were only two ways for me to get free and re-establish a home. I could acquire a Scottish domicile, and then divorce my wife for desertion, or I could let myself be divorced by her under English law. It takes (I think), three years to acquire the rights and privileges of a Scotsman, and it would have meant uprooting myself from Staffordshire, so I finally chose the second alternative.

The Law, which the Church will not allow us politicians to change, insists that a wife shall only be able to divorce her husband if he has been found guilty of desertion and adultery. More merciful than the Church, the Law allows 'desertion' to be assumed if a Writ for the Restitution of Conjugal Rights is obtained and not complied with. So 'letters' were exchanged, and I was duly found guilty of desertion. All the world read in the papers that I had 'deserted' a wife and seven children after twenty years of married life.

Such a thing, if true, strikes me as being more blackguardly than adultery. There was no protest from Mr. Sinker; but I am not likely to forget that day in the House of Commons. I spoke six times that day — on the Education Bill — to a perfectly silent House, feeling that every man was saying: 'That is the man who has deserted his wife and seven children.'

The next stage was to get myself proved guilty of adultery. I chose the simplest way — took a suite of rooms at the Charing Cross Hotel, and took a lady there who was not my wife. As a matter of fact, there was no adultery there. It is not exactly a festive occasion when you are carefully providing evidence to end a happy married life. I cannot imagine what sensible people should expect me to be doing with a sitting-room at a London hotel, except to sleep in, or why anyone who has a comfortable flat in London should go to the Charing Cross Hotel at all. But people who knew that my children were at Moddershall with me, and saw that the 'desertion' conviction must be formal, immediately jumped to the conclusion that the Member for Newcastle was a thorough bad lot, and smacked their lips over 'guilty of adultery'.

I think Mr. Sinker might have been more reticent in the matter, as, had I committed this frightful sin, it would only have been to satisfy the insistence of his Church. And even this avenue to freedom is barred to all but the rich; it has cost me several hundred pounds. Our divorce laws constitute the grossest case of 'one law for the rich and another for the poor'; for which again Mr. Sinker and his kind are responsible.

Throughout, I have done what I conceived to be the most honourable thing in the most honourable way, and I have had good friends to back me up. But I ask you to observe what happens to a public man who tries to act honourably. Out of nine hundred similar cases last year, mine was the only one reported. Three times my portrait was in the picture papers; three times I was deluged in anonymous abuse; three times an honourable name was dragged in the mud, and foremost in the hunt is a minister of the Church of England. I thank the *Sentinel* for taking another line, and for trying to find explanations for what seemed inexplicable.

Whatever my associations may be in the future with those who have honoured me with their confidence for fourteen years, I know that at least they regard me as a man of courage. Under the circumstances, they would not have expected me to do other than I have done. And I have my reward, for before these lines are read, I shall have exercised my right of remarriage, and in that I believe that I shall have the good wishes of all that is best in the county of my birth.

The letter did not remain buried in the columns of *The Staffordshire Evening Sentinel*. Here was an M.P. coolly announcing that he had procured a divorce by conspiracy. Questions were asked in Parliament. There was talk of a prosecution for perjury. But there had been no perjury; the only evidence taken was that of a hotel chambermaid who had seen two pairs of shoes outside a bedroom door. Returning to Westminster Josiah, though a little taken aback at the new publicity, gave as good as he got. The law, he asserted, was not only idiotic but wicked. It created immorality and encouraged dishonesty. Moreover, it made divorce the exclusive prerogative of the rich. The sooner the law was reformed the better for everyone. His point of view found considerable support, however; both in his native county and in the country at large, as the agitation for reform of the divorce laws gathered strength he came in the end to be thought of with gratitude for having struck one of the first and most resounding blows for that cause also.

II

Josiah had not much liked what he saw of the Hungary of Bela Kun. 'I prefer men to cabbages,' he said to one of the government officials who was showing him the achievements of Red Hungary. 'Ah,' said his cicerone, 'I see you are a follower of Bakunin. We believe in Marx.' He always rejected Marxist doctrines, believing steadfastly that the only sound revolution would be achieved in accordance with the views of Henry George, of which he saw no trace in Hungary. 'The dictatorship of the proletariat,' he said at this time, 'is as horrible as the dictatorship of the Caesars.' He was not at all favourably impressed when the official who had been deputed to take him round Budapest dismissed the taxi driver without payment and silenced the poor man's protests by drawing a revolver. Much as he disliked the atmosphere of restraint and apprehension which brooded over Budapest, he felt that people feared rather what they thought the government might do than what it had done. This was not his impression when some years later he went with two other Members of Parliament on an official visit to the Hungary of Horthy, after the counter-revolution and when the so-called officer detachments were carrying on a continuous harrying of the Jews and the Left.

It seemed to me [he wrote to an Hungarian acquaintance] that in Hungary there was little liberty or justice

136

and that all men were afraid. It is very unpleasant to see a
civilized people under the influence of fear . . . Proscription
of political opinion, inability to obtain justice, anti-semitism
in its basest form, crime unpunished, torture condoned —
these things are hateful to a western mind and ought to be
condemned by all decent Magyars. They seem to me to be
accepted — and through fear. A stranger cannot judge of
responsibility. We cannot tell whether the Minister for War
is helpless against the officer detachments or directs them.
We cannot determine the relations of the various parties.
We cannot even be sure that the atrocity stories sworn to
before us are in detail or in gross true, because material for
thorough cross-examination was lacking. But we see people
against whom great and horrible crimes are alleged, free,
honoured and welcomed in Society . . . There were few
civil officials or politicians with whom we spoke who did not
in private deplore and denounce the officer detachments.
But you cannot wash your hands of your country and moral
cowardice is as bad as physical. You can sacrifice yourself
for your country in other ways than by being blown to bits
in No Man's Land; there is always something that can be
done by a man who is not afraid.

Admiral Horthy in an interview admitted that
terrorist gangs were attacking Jews and Leftists, but
confessed himself powerless to stop them. The admission merely convinced Josiah of his fundamental
frivolity and therefore unfitness to rule. A visit to
Bulgaria, where a supposed attempt by revolutionaries
to blow up Sofia cathedral had led to 3000 arrests,
made an equally unfavourable impression. He was
opposed to terrorism and dictatorship of whatever
kind or colour, but in his own experience he found
White Terrors more ruthless, destructive and in-
humane than Red.

Shortly after his return from his first visit to Hungary, in August 1919, he became a member of the

Labour Party where he was in the congenial company
of such old friends as Lansbury and Snowden.

His first major battle was over the reactionary
Aliens Bill in the autumn of 1919. This was for him
the beginning of a fight for the stranger within our
gates which continued for the rest of his life. It is
interesting to find in his earliest speeches on the
subject the same ideas which remained with him to
the end.

At all periods of our history [he said in the House of Commons on October 22nd, 1919] some people have been
opposed to aliens, and have evinced the same spirit that we
have been listening to to-night. Generally speaking, aliens
are always hated by the people of this country. Usually
speaking there has been a mob which has been opposed to
them, but that mob has always had leaders in high places.
The Flemings were persecuted and hunted, and the Lom-
bards were also hunted down by the London mob. Then it
was the turn of the French Protestants. I think that the same
feeling holds good on this subject today. You always have a
mob of entirely uneducated people who will hunt down
foreigners, and you always have people who make use of the
passions of the mob in order to get their own ends politically.
There is behind this amendment a real party movement and
a desire to show on the hustings and platforms what has been
done. Members will come forward and will tell the people,
'I voted against these —— foreigners and I voted to keep
them out.' How men who are English gentlemen can accept
a view of politics that they are to take advantage of the
lowest and meanest ideas of the mob in this country in order
to cadge their votes by such a clause as this, I cannot understand. We have heard hon. members appealing to members
of the Labour party and saying, 'Do you not want more work
for Englishmen and can we not kick out the foreigners and
find work for the men at home?' Although I only speak for a
small section of the Labour party myself we believe that the
interest of the working classes everywhere are the same, and

these people will find it difficult to spread a feeling of animosity and racial hatred amongst those people who realize that the brotherhood of man and the international spirit of the worker is not merely a phrase but a reality. We know that the whole of this bill is devised in order to satisfy the meanest political spirit of the age. If this Amendment were included in the bill it would show what legislation would provide if it were left in the hands of *John Bull* and the hon. member for Ealing, and would let people see that our proud old British traditions had been scrapped and thrown overboard, and that we had invented a new type of English gentleman, modelled on the London mob of 200 years ago.[1]

Clear of his domestic problems, Josiah had new strength for the struggle, for many struggles, and was thoroughly enjoying life. An old hand in debate and at question time, he was constantly on his feet heckling the government — 'an Opposition in himself' as the *Daily Telegraph* not unflatteringly described him. His record for 1919 was 402 questions and speeches running to 230 columns of Hansard.

In the following year he beat his own record at Question time, getting in 456; but he spoke rather less often in debate, a mere 158 columns of Hansard. He was writing at the same time regularly in the Labour weekly *Forward*. Naturally, so determined an individualist found Labour party discipline in some ways more irksome than the easier control of the Liberals. He was soon protesting against the party's regimentation of what its members said in Parliament, and on the question of German reparations he consistently spoke against them. On most questions, however,

---

[1] The Amendment to the Aliens Bill which was under debate had been moved by Sir Ernest Wylde. Its purpose was to limit the number of aliens employed by any single firm and to make all employment of aliens dependent on a licence from the Home Office.

and more especially on India and the Colonies he was at this time wholeheartedly at one with them, and in 1921 he became Vice-Chairman of the Parliamentary Labour Party. It was also during this period that, as the most popular figure in the House, he became generally known to Commons, public and Press by the name of 'Josh', an abbreviation which was, however, repudiated in his family to whom he was always 'Jos'. What excuse is there for blurring the sibilant? People who can turn Jos into Josh will be putting a superfluous 'e' into Wedgwood next.

III

In the three years immediately following the war India was uppermost in his thoughts and interests. It is not possible here to argue the rights and wrongs of the case as it stood between India and the British Raj in the years succeeding the First World War. What weighed with Josiah was principally the dishonour which he felt his country to sustain by a breach of her obligations.

In the heat of controversy — over India, Germany, Russia, aliens or Jews — the uncomprehending or prejudiced will often accuse their opponents of lack of patriotism. This accusation, as his correspondence showed, was often levelled at Josiah. But it accorded extremely ill with his war record, his passionate love of English history and unwavering pride and faith in his country's traditions. He was stirred by the sufferings of the down-trodden, and he felt it his duty as an Englishman to be so stirred. He felt it his duty as an Englishman to protest all the more strongly when an

English government was responsible. He believed that
India should be free and that Indians were suffering
for a good cause; he believed that England had made
offers in the stress of war which the government was
not now prepared to honour, and he felt these broken
pledges as a wound to his own and his country's
honour. His patriotism never burnt more fiercely than
when he was denouncing his country's errors. The
standards he expected Englishmen to reach were high.
As early as 1910 he had vehemently described repressive measures in India as 'treason against our
good name'.

Moreover he believed that India as a free member
of the Commonwealth had a significant part to play.
Already he feared the weakness of the League of
Nations and began to see the Empire as the nucleus of
a new World State for the preservation of peace and
justice among men.

We need the first 'coloured' Dominion as evidence and
proof of what the British Empire stands for in the world —
the first step towards an Indo-British commonwealth of
nations. If we take this road, all the nations of the East will
gradually come in. What they fear is domination and
exploitation. What they need is protection and credit. To
a union in which India is as free as England, all can come
without fear or hestiation. To a union in which India is as
safe as England all might well wish to belong. . . .

In such words he elaborated the vision of an Empire
to which the entire East and Middle East would soon
wish to be joined. But the recognition of India as a
Dominion was the essential first step.

At present, the British Empire is a white Empire with
coloured subject-peoples. It cannot remain so because the
subject-peoples will no longer remain subject. It can shuffle

off the coloured parts and remain a pure white national Empire . . . or it can cease to be a national Empire, and become an International Commonwealth, the germ of world-union. All hangs upon the admission of India as a partner.

With such a vision beginning to form before his eyes, he felt the unrest and violence in India, the massacre at Amritsar and the proclamation of martial law by Sir Michael O'Dwyer in the Punjab as so many wounds to the good name of his country.

He was among that small group of members of Parliament who vehemently condemned O'Dwyer and demanded retributive justice on General Dyer. He was himself in close touch with leaders of Indian opinion especially Lajpat Rai. A letter from Lajpat Rai on conditions in India confirmed what Josiah himself believed, namely that the repressive measures in the Punjab and the violence of the administration were exacerbating and increasing vehement national sentiments.

It is an entirely new India to which I have come back [wrote Lajpat Rai], it is an awakened, self-conscious and defiant India . . . Why don't you come out to India? I think you can do a great service both to the government and the people of India. The people of India have lost all confidence in British justice . . . You know that I would not barter the liberties of my country for anything but I sincerely believe that we cannot afford to have chaos and disorder in our country at this stage of our evolution. There are elements in India who may rise equal to the occasion if any disorder does happen but still I would prefer ordered progress with the certainty of our getting complete responsible government in an India as an integral part of the British Commonwealth in the near future than run the risk of being thrown into a whirlpool of opposing and contending forces. The situation in Western Asia is getting very acute and it

may involve the whole sagacity and might of the British to
ensure order there. No one can say what may happen there.
Of one thing I am certain — that the present policy of
pusillanimity and haggling is the worst. This is the time for
bold things which will appeal to the imagination as well as
the heart of the people of Asia . . . The British are fast losing
their prestige and their influence . . . their Indian advisers
are generally sycophants and their own men lack the breadth
of view and the greatness of heart which characterized the
makers of the Empire. They have been living on prestige
and now that conditions are changing and have changed,
they find it difficult to swallow the pill. It is their pride, their
arrogance, their self sufficiency and their idea of prestige
that will ruin their power in Asia. I say this not in bitterness
but as a friend.

The suggestion that he should come to see for himself was very welcome to Josiah who took the next
possible occasion of doing so.

About eighteen months later he and Florence visited
India. They were received when the ship docked at
Bombay, and thereafter wherever they went, by vast,
enthusiastic crowds. His admirers lassoed him with
garlands and squirted scent on to his white ducks;
once a zealous admirer mistook the bottle and squirted
syrup instead. There were showers of rose-petals,
torchlight processions and fireworks, gratifying
streamers proclaiming 'Welcome Hater of Injustice',
'Welcome Righter of Wrongs'. 'Wedgwood Ki-jai,'
the crowds vociferously shouted, which pleased him
greatly until the bloom of the acclaim was dashed as
they went on to 'Ki-jai' a catalogue of distinguished,
undistinguished and unheard of names. 'It seems that
there are other great men,' he remarked.

He addressed meetings everywhere. In order to
be heard and seen by the smallest in the crowd, he once

climbed on to the table on the platform. The table was ricketty, and his wife was in fear of an ignominious and perhaps painful fall. But all went well. They stayed sometimes at Government House, sometimes with Indian friends. 'We move in a strange world of mixed officials and rebels — seeing and hearing both sides,' he wrote to his mother from Lucknow, and another time:

I have just time for a line of love before I go off for my third interview with Gandhi, the uncrowned King of India. We are leaving this afternoon for the Punjab and Delhi where we shall stop with the Viceroy. I am having the time of my life and doing good work but it is a rush and if it was not for the great kindness of this people I should be dead.

His speeches were many and none of them inflammatory. He spoke of the brotherhood of man, of non-violence, of the hope of a free and united world. At Calcutta he addressed 20,000 people. Later he was present at the All-India Trade Union Congress at Bombay and at one of the earliest meetings of the India National Congress. He preferred on the whole the vigorous Mohammedan to the more passive Hindu, but he capitulated to the sanctity and charm of Gandhi. Yet he disapproved of the Congress policy of non-co-operation, because he believed that it would prevent the formation of a sound democracy. In his view Indian patriots should have taken advantage of the Government of India Act, however disappointing it was in substance and however deeply weakened it had been by the jerrymandering of some of the British authorities. He himself profoundly trusted the intentions of the Government to give Home Rule to India and believed that Indians should in the meantime use the panchayats, or local councils, in order to develop self-government in what he understood as the traditional democratic fashion.

He was also keenly anxious lest, in the bitterness and division of Indian politics and the harshness of the struggle, the fundamental sanity of Parliamentary democracy should be submerged. He was angry and shocked to hear Indians of one party shout down Indians of another. Speaking to Congress at Nagpur he put the matter with his usual vigour:

You cannot expect to hear the truth from your leaders, you cannot expect your leaders to face what they have to face in this country unless you allow more fair play and more freedom of speech. Free speech is the only basis upon which democracy can survive.

I have seen the Irish struggle for independence and I have seen the Boer struggle for independence. Let me tell you that in Ireland the parties were divided far more bitterly than they are in this country. The feeling between the Parnellites and the anti-Parnellites and Mr. O'Brien and Mr. Dillon was far more bitter than between the politicians of this country. But they always behaved to each other like gentlemen and gave one another a patient hearing. Save India from this awful position — that your public men become afraid of public life and retire into private life. I do not know enough about Mr. Jinnah's politics to say whether I agree with him or not, but I do know that a man who has courage to come to this audience and tell you what he has told you, is a man for my respect. The first thing in every political leader is not brains, but courage . . . Let Swaraj be a real Swaraj, democratic Swaraj and not a mobocracy, not the sort of rule that maintained itself in France a hundred and thirty years ago, but a real live passive movement such as your great leader desires and such as he has followed. Follow him not only in passive resistance, but in allowing every minority, however small, to secure justice and fair play in the India of the future.

It was after his tour that he fully developed his new imperial vision in the book he wrote, at the request of Mrs. Besant — *The Indo-British Commonwealth*. His ideas belong, as far as can be judged today, to the number of man's unrealized ideals, yet quotation from them is the fittest comment on his Indian journey and his vision for India:

The object of this book is to show how England can ensure peace by fitting the Empire to become the nucleus of World Union, by becoming herself the centre of a Commonwealth of free peoples enjoying equal rights . . . That can only be obtained by fundamentally reforming the Empire. . . .

Remove gradually the injustice of arbitrary rule, of unequal citizenship, of racial insolence, of opportunities for exploitation. But keep the end in view; that end is Brotherhood. I see no other road to it but the road that is called Democracy, founded upon the belief in the perfectibility of human nature and the predominance already of goodness in mankind.

Yet I would not be too sanguine of success even for democracy. Lenin may be wiser to believe in force directed by Marxian Socialists. Gandhi may be right to base his hopes on Tolstoian anarchy. Democracy seems to me more just than Bolshevism and therefore better. It seems to be more practical than preaching a return to nature's anarchy and relying upon individual conversion.

It will be seen that his political ideas were never isolated but always part of a world-picture, indeed of a world-philosophy.

At the time of his visit to India, it came foremost in his thoughts nor can it ever be said that his interest in Indian liberty diminished. But since in his later years his championship of the Jews was better known to the public, it may be as well to say something more of his relations with India here. He continued through-

out his life to support the cause of Indian independence
and to champion individual leaders of the national
movement, with many of whom he was on terms of
warm friendship. His wife has many memories of
entertaining Indian visitors, distinguished and less
distinguished, at the Ark, and one in particular of a
visit from Mrs. Besant with two Indian disciples
draped in white. At the hour of departure the car
would not start. She had to catch a train for another
meeting. What was to be done? In the steady
drizzle of a wet Staffordshire morning, a ramshackle
car was at length summoned, kindly lent by a neighbouring farmer. There was not room for all inside and
Florence treasures to this day her last vision of Mrs.
Besant, enthroned within the car as it bucked and
snorted along the steep and pitted lane, with a splendid
white-robed figure balanced on each mudboard.

He had hoped that if Labour came to power he
would have some Cabinet post which would enable
him to help India. His ambitions in this respect were
not realized and he was bitterly disappointed by the
cautious attitude to India adopted by the first Labour
Government. Mr. H. S. L. Polak, who had worked
as Gandhi's colleague in championing the South
African Indian Community, tells me that he called
on Josiah at about this time. Josiah showed him a
letter he had drafted to MacDonald tendering his
resignation from the Cabinet as a protest against the
hesitant management of Indian affairs. Mr. Polak,
however, urged him strongly not to send it; he argued
that the resignation of India's known champion from
the Government would only worsen the tension in
Indo-British relations. Josiah accepted the advice and
destroyed the letter. It is difficult to ascertain the
extent of his influence on the Government at this time,

but certainly relations grew slightly easier and a step forward was made by the calling of the First Round Table Conference.

It was on his way home from India that he visited Burma where he also addressed a number of meetings. 'So effective was my oratory,' he wrote later, 'that I retired from Burma after three days with five pairs of slippers, fourteen sunshades and twenty-seven lacquer trays . . . Burma is undoubtedly the country for a Labour M.P. who is thinking of setting up a small business in fancy goods.'

The homeward journey was darkened by anxiety about his mother. On the way out he had stayed some days in Venice and had written reminding her of their Italian tour forty years before and the Venetian beads she used to wear. Several times during the Indian tour, of which he wrote her an almost day-to-day account, he asked whether she wanted him to hurry home, although he would prefer to stay if she could spare him for 'I know I am doing good work'. She was well enough to send on to her friends and family the letters he had written home. Some of them are superscribed 'To be returned very precious', and on one the words have been repeated, in a quavering hand, on the back of the sheet, 'Very precious'.

He reached home three weeks before she died. His politics had often puzzled her and his divorce had distressed her probably more than she admitted, but she had never failed in whole-hearted and intelligent devotion to her son, nor had her pride in him faltered.

IV

In England, meanwhile, the Coalition government was growing unpopular. The post-war boom had turned to slump. Labour gained in strength as distress deepened and unemployment grew. Sir Robert Horne's 'Save-the-trade' Budget — the 'rich man's budget', as the Opposition called it — was vehemently criticized from the Labour benches. Josiah's remedy was a capital levy, the reduction of the tea and sugar duties to release more working-class expenditure and — of course — a more constructive taxation of land in the manner of Henry George. In the Budget debate he argued:

I suggest that in future instead of remitting the Income Tax on agricultural land to one half, instead of remitting the Income Tax on land which is not allowed to be used for agriculture to one sixth, it might be as well to arrange your taxation so that land which was not used was penalized and land which was used had exemption from taxation. In that direction you might find some improvement in production, some improvement in the opportunities for employment, some improvement in the trade of the country. I am confident this Budget will not make things any better. It will give a few more hundreds of pounds to the people who already have got too many hundreds of pounds. It will not relieve unemployment.

In the autumn Lloyd George decided to appeal to the country on the issue of free trade. The election of November 1922 sent the Conservatives to Westminster with a majority of seventy-one over all parties. But Labour's strength had been increased by victories in South Wales, the North, and Clydeside, to 143. The Liberals were gravely reduced. The Conservative government, under Mr. Bonar Law, who resigned owing to ill-health the following spring, faced increasingly difficult times and Mr. Baldwin, who succeeded him, appealed to the country again in the winter of 1923. The session had been marked for Josiah by another unsuccessful attempt to introduce a bill for the Taxation of Land Values.

Both in November 1922 and December 1923 he was returned for Newcastle-under-Lyme by a large majority. In the latter election the Conservatives lost over ninety seats to Liberal and Labour candidates. Strikes and labour troubles were spreading fast and the Government was defeated in January on a vote of confidence. The Labour party, if it could count on Liberal support, believed that it could carry on and Ramsay MacDonald was called to the Palace.

MacDonald had had several weeks to work out his Cabinet as the course of events had been fairly clearly foreseen. Speculation had been busy since Christmas and it was not only among his family and friends that Josiah was tipped for high place. The *Daily News*, the *Daily Herald*, the *Telegraph*, the *Manchester Guardian*, the *Morning Post* and *The Times* mentioned the Colonial Office, the India Office, the Dominions and the Admiralty as likely posts for the activities of Colonel Wedgwood.

These prognostications were not baseless. He was Vice-President of the Parliamentary Labour Party; he was one of its most vigorous speakers and fluent writers. He had a reputation which bridged the Atlantic Ocean and valuable contacts all over the world. He was one of the most popular figures in the House and certainly, at that time, one of the best known public men in England.

But the prophets forgot certain imponderables.

Even before Labour party doctrine hardened into its present dogmatic Socialism, he was very unorthodox. He believed for instance in unrestricted immigration even if it meant the competition of aliens in the British labour market. He had voted against raising the school-leaving age because he disbelieved in compulsion. He had been rightly diagnosed when he visited Hungary as a follower of Bakunin rather than of Marx, but he was above all a follower of Henry George whose doctrines were by this time out of fashion in Labour ranks.

His attitude to party rules was utterly unorthodox, or at least it belonged to an older tradition than that of the disciplined party management which became usual in the twentieth century. To submit to party rules was, he once wrote:

a surrender of conscience, reason and duty which ought to be intolerable to any Member of Parliament. The coercion of these rules . . . sets party before country, force above reason. Debate becomes useless and electors are betrayed.

He always firmly believed in representative government as an essentially personal relationship; the member should offer to his electors his judgment, his conscience and his knowledge, not simply a party label.

He never envisaged the function of the Labour party as that of reform by legislation, or the substitution of State for individual responsibility. To him the beauty of the Henry George system was that it would bring about a fundamental improvement in material conditions by releasing the land in which the livelihood of all is rooted, but would still leave the individual free to make the best of his property or himself. In a letter to *The Times* in 1926 he wrote:

The real business of the Labour party is . . . to put an end to the inferiority complex of the working class, to destroy another slave mentality, to create self-confidence and self respect. Of course the ignorant and feeble clamour for someone else — some State or a Mussolini or a Lenin — to save them. They lap up dependence on others with their mother's milk. The creed of liberty has to be taught as the working class grows older. We manufacture men.

Although he had done as much as any man to build up the morale and fibre of the party, he was already distrusted by many, more especially by the trade unionists to whom his ideas, the outcome of a different kind of education and background, seemed dangerously liberal, in every political and moral sense.

There was one other element in the situation. MacDonald was one of the few men with whom he neither could, nor would, get on, and the dislike was mutual. Josiah never saw any reason for curbing his dislikes or disguising his feelings. It was a mistake for him to yield to his irritation and amuse the readers of *Reynolds' News* with an article entitled 'Should Labour men dine with Duchesses?' Perhaps MacDonald would have had to be more than human to overlook that.

MacDonald, in close co-operation with J. H. Thomas, had planned a cautious Cabinet. In Josiah's view 'all ministers except Snowden were selected by contraries, so that they might know nothing about their subject and cause less trouble to the Departments. "We must not annoy the Civil Service", was the slogan of the first Labour government'. When MacDonald at last sent for him it was only to offer him the very minor post of Financial Secretary to the War Office.

Josiah pointed out that as Vice-Chairman of the Parliamentary Party he could hardly take less than Cabinet rank. 'That is just what is so unfortunate,' said MacDonald ungraciously, 'however, I will see what I can do for you.' He made him Chancellor of the Duchy of Lancaster. It was a deflationary conclusion to the happiest years of his Parliamentary life.

In so far as his hopes had been fixed on playing a part in the government of his country, his career was virtually over in 1924. The first Labour government had a short life chequered with rising industrial troubles. He was given the unpopular appointment of Chief Civil Commissioner to deal with emergencies arising from industrial disputes. His task was to ensure the fuel and water services in case of widespread strikes, a post which was bound, if such a crisis occurred, to make him unpopular with both sides.

One minor incident must, or so I like to think, have given him pleasure. He took part in an unusual, if small, historic occasion. It so happened that in Goodwood week it became essential for the King to call a Privy Council in order to confirm a legal decision relative to the Northern Irish frontier. These occasions are a necessary formality, the legal members of the Privy Council having first reached their decision which cannot, however, have the force of law until the King has consented. In general there is no great hurry, but on this occasion time was important. Josiah — not a racing man — was called to Goodwood House with Sir Hugh (now Lord) Macmillan (to whom I am indebted for this interesting detail). Two racing peers were summoned to complete the quorum and King George V uttered the essential words. This meeting of the Privy Council in a private house is unique in the last two centuries.

Very soon after the unstable Government fell. The election was fought in the heated atmosphere caused by the publication of the Zinoviev letter. In the Labour collapse Josiah preserved his seat at Newcastle, though with a reduced majority. Shortly after he was elected to the executive of a chastened Labour party. He did not wish to be nominated again in the succeeding year as he was already feeling the loss of his freedom to criticize, but he allowed himself to be overpersuaded, accepted nomination for election for another term and was voted out of the executive after all.

Free to criticize again, he fought — as he did to the end — a spirited rearguard action over the Taxation of Land Values. To this period belongs the letter that he wrote in answer to an attack in the extreme Socialist weekly *Forward:*

Yes! my dear Tom, Liberty *is* 'the Right to do as we like'. You have a perfect right, if you like, to put an 'e' in the middle of my name. It is anti-social; it is even mistaken; but I do not propose to call in the police. I hope you will learn better. Just as I hope mankind will learn better — to like doing things which do not hurt others.

I believe in the perfectibility of human nature. You do not. That alone, if we lived in the 16th century, would have forced us to burn one another alive. Our ancestors were most imperfect gents, but resolute.

Every time I see a policeman taken off duty I rejoice. Every time you see a fresh one put on you say, 'This is Socialism in our time. Hallelujah!'

By Socialism, I suppose you mean Social Reform and inspecting babies' hair. By Socialism I mean a land (or a time), when we shall not need policemen. We are getting rid of armies. Even you believe that they are out of date. You love authority. I love freedom. Quite recently men shot one another for less. But the real unsurmountable barrier between us is, that you will not see *why* we need policemen at present, or what purpose they really serve.

In the present struggle for life we need police, because in that struggle men become fierce brutes. And we struggle for life because 'the police' will not let us use the land that is necessary for life — or, at least, not use enough of it.

But having explained how utterly I differ from you and all your kidney, and how delighted I shall be to hate you, let me end with the same amiabilities which grace your outburst.

I, too, find you 'likeable'; and that because we have one other great difference (I trust only temporary). I have long since found the truth. You, alone of your colleagues are still courageously looking for it.

Yours quite cordially,

Josiah C. Wedgwood.

At the Labour Party Conference at Margate in 1926 he strongly attacked the party policy on agriculture, emphasizing with truth that until they had a programme that appealed to the agricultural labourer as well as to the town worker they would never be in a position to gain more than very partial working-class support. He still believed that the movement for the taxation of land values, which as he saw it was the safe and logical way to free the land for the people, was 'the last and greatest of the liberation movements'. This belief no longer commanded support in any political party. One by one those who had stood with him in the abundantly hopeful days of 1910 had died or abandoned their views — even his admired friend Philip Snowden when he came to introduce a Land Valuation Bill failed to live up to the principles of Henry George.

A land policy based on Georgite doctrine was also the foundation of his attitude towards colonial development. He abhorred and persistently attacked the policy which, in West Africa for instance, was creating a landless proletariat so as to compel the native to work. Such exploitation even if it produced wealth, a raised standard of living, and social services, seemed to him the negation of justice, a thing wrong in itself and evil in its outcome. His own work in Nigeria had laid a very different foundation.

When Labour came into power again in the summer of 1929 MacDonald did not offer him a seat in the Cabinet. 'There are no jobs coming my way,' he wrote to Ralph while the Cabinet was being formed, 'but I cannot feel myself aggrieved as I have long been aware of the sentiments regarding myself held by the good MacDonald. I can survive and as Winston said to me last night "move a little to the left".'

Two years later he refused to sign the pledge of obedience to discipline which the Labour party imposed on its members. He gave his reasons in a letter to his old friend George Lansbury.

Dear Lansbury,

This is the undertaking you ask me to sign before I can be considered a member of the Parliamentary Labour party in this Parliament. Needless to say, it has never been asked of any of us before. Charles Trevelyan and Fred Jowett refused to sign it, and I cannot think how you and Attlee could bring yourselves to do so. For the undertaking is dishonourable as well as being the negation of democracy. No man, save in the Church of Rome, can so far divest himself of Freedom and responsibility:

I undertake to accept and act in harmony with the standing orders of the Parliamentary Labour Party. Any candidate who, after election, fails to accept or act in harmony with the Standing Orders shall be considered to have violated the terms.

I gathered from your talk with me that you did not fully realize the implications of these standing orders.

(1) In the somewhat rare case of a decision by the party meeting as to how the party shall vote in the House, no M.P. may vote contrary to the decision. If his objection is conscientious he may absent himself from the division, and conscience is understood to cover views on drink as well as views on religion, but not pledges given to electors.

(2) In the great majority of cases there is no party decision as to how we shall vote. In all such cases the party Whips decide the matter, no doubt after consultation with any leader available. But whatever pledges have been given to constituents, no more latitude than stated above is allowed by the standing order. And by the undertaking you ask me to sign, any breach of the standing order becomes, not a political risk, but a breach of honour.

(3) No notice of motion, reduction of vote, or amendment may be moved or put upon the paper without the previous sanction of the Chief Whip or party meeting. Even questions are discouraged and only permitted on sufferance.

These standing orders turn a Member of Parliament into a voting dummy, and they throw the whole Labour movement open to ridicule. Self-respecting men will decline to stand for Parliament in our interest. But the real implication, which you do not see, is far more serious than any effect upon the independence of members or the fortunes of a party.

In old days Members of Parliament were very particular to conceal from the electors what they did in Parliament — how they carried out their pledges. They objected to any publication of speech or vote. But for two hundred years, in the interest of honesty and of democracy, we have allowed records of speeches and votes. Our names are taken down as we pass the turnstile that we may be held responsible, that we may be judged.

But the party meeting is secret; no record of how you vote there, and to divulge is held to be dishonourable. In future the electorate have no hold upon the member. 'Why did you vote "Aye"?' 'Because the party decided so, and we must obey the majority of the party.' 'How did you vote at the party meeting?' 'That is secret, and I am bound in honour not to tell you.' So the man can make any pledge and break any pledge, and shelter all the time behind the party, leaving the party to take the blame. It is a coward's protection order, and divisional Labour parties would do well to refuse adoption to those who consent to sign. I do beg you to get these standing orders liberalized, and the honour-compelling undertaking withdrawn. I ask it not for my sake, nor because you as well as I (quite good elements for any party to include) often broke such standing orders in the past. But I ask you for the sake of the traditions and dignity of this House of Commons of ours.

The order is for the convenience and authority of leaders. But Labour members are as anxious as are members of other parties to stand well with their leaders — to get the jobs and honours, and career, and trips abroad. It is as easy for you as for other leaders to secure sufficient discipline. I cannot believe that an autocracy never tolerated in any other party in England (except the Communist) is essential to keep private members straight — or to give some leaders liberty to go crooked.

For old times' sake he never withdrew from the party, although his beliefs were more and more at variance with theirs as doctrinaire Socialism gained ground. But he never lost his faith in Labour or the hope — which he did not live to see realized — that Labour only would give freedom to India.

Such in its bare outline was the end of his ambition for the wielding of political power. It would be absurd to deny that he had cherished, until the early nineteen-twenties, a not unreasonable hope that he might set his mark on history, and especially on the development of the Empire, as a progressive statesman at the Colonial or the Dominions Office.

Two lines of conduct are open to the man who finds the progress of his just ambition suddenly checked. He can become an embittered might-have-been, or he can abandon his ambition and set his course for a different shore. The second and wiser course is easier to recommend than to follow. Josiah had the strength of character, the resilience, and the zest for life which made it possible for him to follow it.

A leader other than MacDonald might have retained him more effectively within the party. There were some who keenly felt that one of their best men was being wasted. He was among the strongest personalities of the party and in the years which followed the Labour collapse of 1931 it could have done with some strong personalities. In his memoirs Lord Strabolgi, writing in 1933, goes so far as to suggest that he 'would have made a far better leader than MacDonald from 1924 to 1929'. A more adventurous one, anyway. He would have led any party, one feels, on the principle of daring to put it to the touch to gain or lose it all. This is not a popular principle with elder statesmen.

The advent of Clement Attlee as leader of the party undoubtedly cast a glow of returning hope for Labour over the last years of Josiah's life in the Commons. He admired him greatly, 'He is far and away the best leader the Labour party has had or could have. In the first place he is a better read man than any other in Parliament in my time ... he has the highest standards which free him from both ambition and selfishness. I have never heard him depreciate a colleague. In every respect he is the exact antithesis of MacDonald. Nobody is afraid of him or for him: all like him.'

I owe to Mr. Attlee a story which is significant of

the way in which Josiah would sink his views if he was
approached by someone for whom he had respect. Mr.
Attlee writes:

> I worked with him in Committee upstairs on the De-
> rating Bill in the 1924 Parliament. Before it came down for
> Report stage, Josh had fallen foul of our Front Bench. They
> made too many agreements with the enemy. He would go
> to the back benches and lead the irregulars. However, when
> the Derating Bill came downstairs, Josh agreed to come back
> to the Front Bench to lead the fight. I wandered in after
> dinner to see how it was getting on. 'It's all right,' said
> Josh, 'I've fixed up everything. It will be through by nine
> o'clock.'

But for the last nineteen years of his life he made the
best of his position as a free agent, untrammelled by
party ties, political caution or hope of office. He could
now play a lone hand for the causes in which he believed. An article in the *Daily Herald* had described
him once as 'the Knight-errant of our politics, the
champion of all those who can reward him only with
a place in their prayers, the generous foe, the un-
wearied friend, the Happy Warrior'. His Knight-
errantry had played its part in building up the reputation of the Labour party in Parliament from 1919 to
1924.

For the last twenty years of his life he skirmished
valiantly on the wings, championing oppressed minorities, subject races, persecuted individuals, saying things
about policy which cannot always be said within the
framework of party and asking questions which ought
to be asked by someone but cannot be asked by the
'responsible'. As evening fell it may sometimes have
seemed to onlookers as though the lengthening shadow
of the Knight-errant resembled that of a famous

Spanish Knight. In the night and storm of the 'thirties it was not always easy, for those who kept the faith, to tell what were windmills and what were giants. But there were more giants than windmills, and to some of the giants his good lance gave a mortal wound.

CHAPTER VII

HISTORY AND LITERATURE

D URING these active years in Parliament, Josiah had found time to pursue his researches into the past. History had always been his favourite spare-time reading and local history his favourite hobby. He had joined the William Salt Archaeological Society (since re-named the Staffordshire Record Society) as soon as he came back from South Africa, served for many years on its committee and efficiently filled the post of honorary secretary. Possibly owing to his interest in Land Values he was fascinated with late medieval land tenure and would talk about virgates with the same shining look in his eyes that came when he talked of Poitiers or Dunbar.

The development of the local industry was another favourite subject of his. Soon after he came back to his native country he decided to compile a history of Staffordshire pottery. The book, which was the result of several years of interrupted, but careful, research, was published in August 1922 under the title of *Staffordshire Pottery and its History*. It had a respectful press and is still regarded as a standard work on the subject. He dedicated it to 'my constituents who do the work'.

The book was intended for the general public, or it would be truer to say for such of the general public as are interested in the history of pottery. He had published some years before, for private circulation only, the first results of his genealogical researches in the form of a massive family history. A little later he was to publish, also for private circulation, a contribution to family history of a more unusual kind. He had established the small but not uninteresting fact that only one place in England is called Wedgwood, a farm near Brindley Ford in North Staffordshire. Its owners somewhere in the fourteenth century adopted its name as a patronymic in the usual medieval fashion. 'Wedgwood is an early established surname,' wrote Josiah, 'yet we can trace it to the very origin. We might know the relationship of every Wedgwood. There are none who can come from anywhere else for there was no such place elsewhere to come from. We have the lot in one ring-fenced family.'

What he set out to do in his volume of *Wedgwood Pedigrees*, privately published in 1925, was to trace 'the lot'; to herd all the sheep he could find bearing the name into one pen and see what they added up to. Difficulties about variant spellings and derived forms of the name he solved in his usual cut-the-knot style:

The name has been spelt in precisely 198 different ways, from Weadghewode to Wegvud, from Widgewoode to Widgett, and the Widgett cousins I have not sought to trace. People who would permit such a degradation are better forgotten. Our pottery branch and the New Englanders have never varied in the spelling since 1616, always Wedgwood. But many of the Yorkshire colony (which left Staffordshire about 1650) insist on a second 'e'; the Darlington clothiers are still Wedgewood & Sons, and I am told the stove-maker of San Francisco puts Wedgewood on his otherwise excellent stoves ... To the lack of orthographical precision in our name we may no doubt attribute the lack of such pedantic precision in the daily correspondence of the modern representatives. Why should Wedgwoods spell correctly?

The resulting book is no glorious account of a family

privileged and honoured, bearing coat armour and amassing titles. It is a register — not complete but surprisingly full — of a very typical English middle-class family: middle class, that is, by origin, for much of the book is given over to the record of the submerged or partially submerged branches, the younger sons of younger sons whose enormous families of short-lived children were born and died in the murk of industrial back streets and the shadow of the factory. For the social historian the book is a document of some interest if only because there is not, so far as I know, another work which follows the holders of a common surname through so many peculiar and otherwise unrelated ramifications.

Josiah's life in Parliament, his interest in Stafford-shire, in history and in genealogical research have only to be added together to explain why his next work was an account of Staffordshire M.P.s from the beginnings of Parliament to the Reform Bill. This is a major historical work of its kind and may be consulted in three volumes, published in their *Collections for the History of Staffordshire* by the William Salt Archaeological Society.

For the non-historian it may be necessary to say something here about the significance of Parliamentary history and of the biographies of members in particular. In spite of generations of research there are many questions on the past history of our institutions to which we can give only tentative answers. A country with very ancient institutions is often tempted to read back into their past, characteristics which are typical of their present state only. Of no institution is this more true than of the English Parliament which has shown a Protean capacity for change and growth during its seven centuries of life. One way of investigating the past of an institution is to inquire into the identity of the people who composed it.

When he set to work to trace the lives of Staffordshire M.P.s, Josiah had no idea in his mind beyond that of filling in the gap in the history of his own county. But his devotion to Parliament as an institution and his belief in it went beyond the bounds of mere local interest. A passage from the introduction to his volumes on the Staffordshire M.P.s sums up his deeper feelings:

To me, personally, Parliament is everything; the members are the staunchest friends a man ever had; the life combines the mental gymnastics of college with the fresh wind of the outer world; only the recesses are intervals of stagnation. There is no other Parliament like the English. For the ordinary man elected to any senate, from Persia to Peru, there may be a certain satisfaction in being elected. He is to be at least among the rulers; the plaudits of supporters are in his ears; he has the envious admiration of his old associates; perhaps even nobler aspirations may be gratified. But the man who steps into the English Parliament takes his place in a pageant that has ever been filing by since the birth of English history. Men with long swords and short daggers were his predecessors, as they rode to Westminster over Dunsmore Heath, drinking ale in the taverns of Coventry and Towcester. Men with spiked shoon disputed loudly, in the terms he still uses, about the insolence of York and the profusion of Warwick. In slashed breeches and ruffled collars they denounced the Bishop of Rome and clamoured for the internment of all recusants. 'The country was going to the dogs' under Cromwell just as it was under Gladstone, as the members walked two and two into a Palace Yard that was 'new' in 1600, or called for torches or 'who goes home?' York or Lancaster, Protestant or Catholic, Court or Country, Roundhead or Cavalier, Whig or Tory, Liberal or Conservative, Labour or Unionist, they all fit into that long pageant that no other country in the world can show. And they one and all pass on the same inextinguishable torch — burning brightly or flickering — to the next man in the race, while freedom and experience ever grow. These men who have gone by, who have had the glimmer of the torch on them for a little time, are those whose memories I want to rescue, and in so doing reincarnate a small section of the Parliaments which made us.

In other less dramatic passages, he indicated the nature of his views and standards. Among the Elizabethan M.P.s there was Thomas Fitzherbert who bribed Elizabeth's villainous chancellor Topcliffe to get rid of most of his relations on the scaffold. Topcliffe, Josiah wrote, has been described as 'a monster of iniquity' but, he goes on, 'the English language is quite unable to cope with Thomas Fitzherbert'.

During the 'twenties his mind turned more and more to the idea of a great Parliamentary history. As he watched the political scene he grew early aware of the threat to democracy. Although his sympathies were with the Left he did not like the dictatorial methods of the Left revolutions. When he took the chair for 'Red' Emma Goldman on her visit to England in 1925 he spoke with some vehemence of the growing tyranny in Russia, remarks which cannot have been welcome to that particular audience. The Fascist Revolution in Italy filled him with foreboding and he would never accept the comforting belief that 'Italy was different'. The thing, he rightly saw, was a portent. His reactions to the dictatorships in Hungary and Bulgaria have already been discussed. Thus, long before most people began to see Great Britain as a stronghold of Parliamentary democracy in a world of authoritarianism, he had seen his country in this way.

His was not a mind neatly divided into partitions,

one for history, one for politics, one for the philosophy of life; with him, everything moved together. The inspiration which had carried him through long months of persistent, if interrupted, research into Staffordshire M.P.s was not purely a scholarly inspiration; he was recording and vindicating a great institution and the history of his country. Political development in Europe was a major incentive to his now growing ambition to sponsor a Parliamentary history on the lines of the *Dictionary of National Biography*.

At first all went well with this truly magnificent plan. In May 1928 he began to organize a petition to the Prime Minister and within a few months had collected the signatures of 400 Members of Parliament and forty peers, asking that the need for such a work should be taken into public consideration. In the following March a Committee was appointed under his chairmanship to consider the whole question. Two and a half years were spent in collecting evidence and consulting with historians from both sides of the Atlantic. Professors Namier (Manchester), Notestein (Yale), and Neale (London) — all names to conjure with where Parliament is concerned — were the three chief advisers: the three Ns, as Josiah thought of them. Professor A. F. Pollard, author of the great *Evolution of Parliament*, was also of the Committee.

The Interim Report appeared in July 1932. This remarkably interesting document strongly advocated that the work of compiling a full record of Parliament, consisting of the biographies of members and a reconstruction of procedure, should be set on foot. The language of the Report in explaining the significance of the work is smoother and more impersonal than any that Josiah would have used writing from the heat of his feelings alone; but it shows that he had at that time breathed his spirit into the Committee.

An institution has its foundations in the past, and at any moment in its history can only be understood through a knowledge of the past. The causes of its weaknesses, no less than of its strength, can only be diagnosed with sureness in the light of diagnoses of the past; and knowledge of the way in which various forces have modified its character and utility in former times will open our eyes to the operation of forces today, to which otherwise we would almost certainly be blind.

Moreover there is some danger of Parliament losing its dignity and prestige even in our own country. A wider franchise has tended to exclude from public life, both in the House of Commons and in municipal councils, many public-spirited people whose unwillingness any longer to take part in government is a loss to the State. To give members a sense of their community in a famous inheritance might do much to restore the dignity of their service. Universities, inns of court, schools and other institutions have long been aware of this. 'People will not look forward to posterity, who never look backward to their ancestors.'

The prestige of Parliament itself is a thing to be cared for at a time when Parliaments are being broken in other countries. We celebrate at the same time the centenary of the Reform Bill and the fourth centenary of the Reformation Parliament, and remember that 'many men have gone about to break Parliament but, in the end, Parliament has broken them'.

Unfortunately the financial crisis of 1931 had intervened and the Committee had to be dissolved. Josiah and some of his fellow enthusiasts, however, now set to work to raise the necessary funds by private subscription and in 1934 the Government, impressed by the growing response, guaranteed to put up one half of the money (£30,000 was the estimated total cost of the scheme), if the other half could be raised by subscription. Josiah, who was already at work on certain parts of the history with a number of volunteers (*quorum pars minima fui*) threw himself with redoubled vigour into the business of raising the money. He wrote to the Press; he enlisted American help; he circularized M.P.s. The Pilgrim Trust had already given £2000. His enthusiasm and energy were boundless. He himself had already all but finished — with the help of that good historian and good Liberal Anne Holt — the volume on the Wars of the Roses, always his favourite epoch.

Meanwhile he had a little private fun with the modern volume which he had added to the scheme partly as a bait to draw in living M.P.s to subscribe. In order to compile this he circularized all M.P.s with a questionnaire of his own devising. The great quiz fashion had not then set in, and a number of the stuffier members were incensed at being suddenly presented by the outrageous Colonel Wedgwood with a request to fill in answers to such questions as: 'What were your religious convictions at 21?' 'What was your annual income, earned or unearned, when you first stood for Parliament?' MacDonald declared furiously that the questions were inquisitorial and impertinent. Josiah sent them to Snowden with the message, 'Ramsay says I am no gentleman, so I am sure you will answer the questions.' Snowden sent back his answers, but added a light-hearted postscript, 'This is the only time in my life when I have agreed with Ramsay.' An extra question — 'Why have you failed?' — was added only to great friends, for, after all, as Josiah argued, most men fail in gaining the ambitions of their youth. Of those who answered this one, I believe only Lord Beaverbrook, with the utmost firmness and good humour, declared that he had *not* failed.

During the years which had passed since Josiah first launched his scheme much had changed. The European scene had deeply darkened. The collapse of the Weimar Republic and the onward march of Fascism was the background against which he was now planning his great scheme. Undoubtedly he brought to it wider considerations than those of historical research; it was to be a monument to the growth of Parliamentary democracy. This caused him to view with profound distrust the attack on the 'Whig interpretation' of English history by the younger scholars of the twentieth century.

Trouble began to arise almost as soon as it became necessary to appeal for subscriptions. In order to make the work more generally attractive, it was decided to include, as well as biographies of M.P.s and lists of Parliaments, a volume of conclusions with each period. Over the nature of these conclusions Josiah's views sometimes came into collision with the more ruthlessly inquiring and sometimes necessarily iconoclastic attitude of the scholars. In his report some years later Lord Macmillan has very fairly stated the case:

> Many important questions, on which opinion among historians is sharply divided, would have to be dealt with, and an authoritative declaration made on matters which are still under debate among historians and which from the nature of the evidence may never be finally decided.

The necessary money was meanwhile raised and the first two volumes of the monumental work were published in 1936 and 1938. Inevitably in the circumstances there was a good deal of criticism, to which Josiah replied with unabated fighting skill. But his fighting skill was in demand on other fronts as well, for war was now fast approaching, and the suspension

THE LAST OF THE RADICALS

of the work seemed probable. In 1940 the quarrel was settled by the formation of a History of Parliament Trust in whose hands the incomplete fragments of the Parliamentary History remained until 1951, when, thanks to the efforts of Lord Macmillan and Sir Frank Stenton, the great work was resumed.

Shortly after the formation of the Trust, Lord Macmillan issued a report on the state of the work to which I cannot do better than refer all those who are interested. It gives the whole story of the venture in brief with justice to all parties. Josiah writing to thank its author described it as 'a most kind and soothing — and even truthful report'. He added a last word of mingled pride and apology: 'My begging letters (to M.P.s) always insisted on the importance of keeping up the standard of recruits for Parliament by giving them a touch of immortality.'

It would give a wrong impression to end this account of Josiah's career as historian and man of letters on this unhappy tale of discord. His interest in local antiquities had soon led him into contact with the Place-name society of which he was for many years a member and for some time treasurer. To this body of learned men and women he was known only as the most genial and helpful of colleagues.

His kindness and encouragement to young students, or to those who brought new knowledge to his attention, was unstinted. He was without jealousy in his researches and his unwillingness to accept certain points of view in history which differed from his own was prompted by the passionate intensity of his political principles, never by any personal animosity towards those who held them.

He had a particular affection and respect for American scholars, seeing in America generally the great inheritor of the best in European traditions. As well as the great Professor Notestein, the dean of American seventeenth-century studies, I used often to meet young American scholars at his office or more convivially at tea on the terrace. On at least one occasion he came forward to champion with the warmest enthusiasm the work of an American editor, Mr. W. H. Dunham of Yale, against the criticisms of English scholars. Mr. Dunham was working in Josiah's favourite fifteenth century on his edition of the Fane Fragment, an early copy of a House of Lords Journal of 1461 the earliest known date for such a journal to exist in any form. With typical enthusiasm Josiah gave interviews to the Press on this significant discovery, advertised it to his historically-minded colleagues in the House of Commons and entered the lists to break a lance with no less a scholar than the late Professor Pollard. This kind of wholehearted championship was heart-warming both to experience and to watch. For his friendship, enthusiasm and kindness he will be long and gratefully remembered by many.

I I

Apart from history, he poured out through the whole course of his life a stream of articles on political subjects — India, Zionism and the Taxation of Land Values, Marxism, Palestine and the Taxation of Land Values, Labour problems, depressed areas, Mr. Gandhi, and the Taxation of Land Values. His output was more or less continuous for the twenty years succeeding the first world war, mostly in such papers as

Forward, Clarion, Reynolds', the *Herald* and the *Nation.*
Some of his earlier pieces he collected in his *Essays and
Adventures of a Labour M.P.*, published in 1924. Parts
of others were incorporated in his vigorous *Memoirs of
a Fighting Life* (1940) to which this book owes much.
Two more books followed.

One of these was a collection of prose and verse,
Forever Freedom. He had projected it with A. P. Herbert in 1938, but he completed it during the war with
the help of Allan Nevins. The book which was published as a 'Pelican' in 1940 was intended as an anthology of the literature of liberty, common to both Great
Britain and America. It was intended, he explained
in a letter to his daughter Camilla, 'to teach English
to foreigners and freedom to English children'. The
anthology is for its purpose a very good one and its
purpose, or at least his description of it, casts some
light on his opinions and illumines in retrospect one
aspect of the quarrel over Parliamentary history. This
was how Josiah introduced the book:

When I exhort my electors, or any Labour audience, to
abhor Fascism and to remain 'faithful to death to your
freedom and laws', I am conscious of a certain strain. Liberty
is not obvious in their everyday life as in mine; it has not
been stressed in their education; they are not familiar from
childhood with what is in this book. Though all my Labour
colleagues regard Socialism as merely a stage on the road
to that economic freedom which is our common goal, yet
dependence on the State ever grows. A new master replaces
the old masters. The mountain top is obscured and those
who have no vision tend to become willing cogs in the new
bureaucratic machine. This machine, the scaffolding of
life, becomes a God whom it is blasphemy to criticize and
criminal to obstruct.

Moreover, the obscuring of the Celestial City of Liberty

HISTORY AND LITERATURE

has affected all the teaching of history. The new history blackens England's past in an endeavour to belittle liberalism and exalt authority. . . .

That was what he had feared and disliked most of all in the outlook of the rising generation of history students with whom he had come into contact. It was the fear that they meant to pull down the old libertarian theory of English history that had made him fight so hard to maintain control, in his own way, over the History of Parliament.

The secondary purpose of *Forever Freedom* was to demonstrate the parallel traditions of England and America, traditions rooted in language and literature.

A common language gives us a common literature, and a common literature gives old and young common ideals. It is not merely that a Mark Twain or a Macaulay gives us a common idea of what is right, gives Britain and America a common religion, a common loathing of cruelty, for instance. They also give to children of all sorts common quotations, common familiarities for all the rest of their lives. The *Bab Ballads, Uncle Remus, Alice in Wonderland, Huck Finn* and the *Lays of Ancient Rome*, furnish both sides of the Atlantic with masonic passwords — quotations that can always be recognized by the elect, and please the elect by taking them all back to a common childhood.

Common nonsense is a surer tie than common sense.

Perhaps he overestimated the education and the memories of most men. Perhaps his choice of books in this passage is old-fashioned or idiosyncratic. But the general meaning stands. There is much truth in it.

Six months before his death he published his last book, *Testament to Democracy*. By that time he must have known that he had not long to live. He was just seventy but for the last twelve years he had been subject to heart attacks of increasing severity and he refused to lead the less strenuous life that might have prevented their recurrence. He therefore put into this book everything which he urgently felt should be brought before men's minds in the crisis through which Europe was passing.

'Fascism and the Corporative State direct the fashionable whirlwind and fancy they can guide the storm into a planned world,' he wrote. Both Fascism and the planned world were anathema to him; to him the virtue of government was to be judged by how far it 'enables the governed to do without it, enables the subject to become a master, a self-respecting citizen; the mob to acquire judgment and conscience; the selfish to respect the rights of others; the animal to become divine; the wise man to emerge who shall need no coercion to deal honestly, humanly and justly by his fellows.'

For him the chief function of Parliament was not to legislate but to control the executive, a point of view which would have been fully shared by John Pym, John Hampden, and a number of his other heroes. As he saw the situation in the middle of the twentieth century, Parliament was lamentably failing in this duty which the Press had (fortunately) usurped from its nerveless hands. 'Newspaper editors have stood up to their proprietors,' he wrote, 'much better than have Members of Parliament to their Government.' He put down this sad decline to two developments: the growth

of rigid party discipline and the ever-increasing number of junior ministerial appointments which in effect
silence criticism of the Government among the bright
young men of the party — the very group from which,
if out of office, the most stimulating criticism could be
expected. Defying the party was, in Josiah's view, an
important part of the ordinary member's duty. 'A
free Parliament,' he declared, 'is not a machine for
making laws; it is a machine for preventing Government from making laws.' This point of view, which
grows more remote and extraordinary year by year
as Parliament declines into a mechanism for legislating, is one of which we should not lose sight. Parliament, at its most influential moments, has so acted.
It would do no harm if its members were to keep that
interesting historic fact in mind.

He feared, rightly, the decline of democracy owing
to ignorance of its principles. 'While Liberal and
Labour are both pledged vaguely to democracy,' he
wrote, 'parents find it difficult to explain its virtues to
their children. It is much easier to explain benevolent
socialism, which has more in common with Christian
communism than with the "good old cause".' As he
grew older he knew himself to be more and more alone
in his idealist belief that in some future, but approaching time, man would be too intelligent to need many
laws. Yet he held manfully to the hope, condemned
paternal government, and believed that, in states like
Great Britain at any rate, compulsory education would
soon be unnecessary because it would be unthinkable
that any parent should not send his child to school.
Certain other deliberate oddities he kept in his book
because, as he explained to his brother Ralph who
had suggested modifications, 'at seventy one may as well
remain honest, trust in reason, and state the argument'.

The book was written in the hurly-burly of war; it had replaced another — on the joint and parallel traditions of freedom of Great Britain and the United States — the notes for which had been lost when the boat which was bringing his luggage back from America went down. Perhaps, had he lived longer, he would have written that as well. As things happened the book entitled his *Testament* was what he had half conceived that it might be, a political testament for any like-minded men who should come after him — if any there were.

The book was published in the last months of his life and during one of the hardest moments of the war but it was received with warmth and widely read. Among those who reviewed it was Professor Namier with whom Josiah had had some bitter arguments when the Great Schism occurred in the Parliamentary History. Professor Namier's words of welcome to this book came from the heart. They also contained what is surely a message, an olive-branch, for the author to read between the lines. He could not give his old friend full marks for precision and scholarly accuracy but he wrote:

a light burns at the centre, a fire more valuable than logic and precision and far more sacred than mere intellectual achievements. Well-framed argument, carefully tested and marshalled facts and fool-proof statement can provide the hard shell for truth but truth itself springs from the human heart, from the depth of human emotions. Jos's truth often lacked the shell which should protect the kernel: but how much superior is he to those whose hard polished shells encompass a void or cover a shrivelled, decaying core.

It was, I think, only the rapid advance of his last illness which prevented Josiah from responding to these words of affection, and re-knitting the bonds of an old friendship.

The happy warrior had many quarrels, literary, historical and political, but he had no lasting enemies.

CHAPTER VIII

ZIONISM

THE English of the old Puritan stock have much in common with the Jew. They have traditions rooted in the Old Testament from which they often draw their first names. The Old Testament as understood by the men of the seventeenth century and their descendants is, of course, rather different from the Old Testament of the practising Jew; and there is no Talmud in the Puritan tradition. But there is the basis of a common attitude to morality, a certain mutual respect and understanding. Josiah summed it up in his reflections on 'The Seventh Dominion' in the days when he hoped that Palestine, 'the Clapham Junction of the Commonwealth', might be that Seventh Dominion.

The Anglo-Saxon, more than any other race, wants to sympathize with the Jew, and would like to settle up for these last 2000 years. They would like to get on to terms of mutual respect; they have for Jews a sort of affection which is perhaps a little patronizing and just a little nervous — of their brains. We both are moneylenders and unpopular; we, too, are wanderers among strange peoples; we, too, are traders, and if we rather look down on those with whom we trade, that is only what the Jews do too. We, too, find in the Old Testament, or Torah, convenient justification for all that needs justification in our relations with mankind. We, too, can laugh at ourselves, so sure are we of being in reality the Chosen People. Having all these tastes in common, no doubt we understand the Jew better than can those to whom the Old Testament is not familiar from infancy. To the foreigner the word Jew is a hissing in the street; to us the word suggests Solomon and Moses, and a thousand cradle stories. So often have we used their names for our own children that they seem now to be our fathers, specially our Puritan forefathers, of whom we can only remember that which was good. When my ancestors hewed down the aristocrats at Wigan Lane and at Naseby they were armed with the names of Aaron and of Abner; and they rallied to the charge, calling on the God of Israel in the language of the prophets.

The nascent Jewish struggle for a new nation was not, I think, known to him before the first world war. The night he landed from the *River Clyde* the Zionist Mule Corps was just alongside. They lent him five mules to carry some of his guns. He admired their fighting spirit, recalling vaguely the Maccabees — who were his favourite Jews although, strictly speaking, they are outside the Old Testament.

Dorothy Richardson first told him of the theory of Zionism some months later in London. For two reasons he thought it was a magnificent idea. Strategically, an efficient state in Palestine, friendly to Great Britain, and preferably a Dominion of the Commonwealth, would have evident advantages. Morally, he believed that special virtues came from the confidence of nationality.

The object of Zionism [he wrote] is to increase, perhaps create, the self-respect of a scattered and submerged race. The supreme work of statesmanship, or of philosophy, is to raise man's self-respect. All virtues come therefrom. . . .

Zionism will give peace and justice as well as pride to the Jews, both of Palestine and of the Diaspora, after two thousand years.

Years later when he was talking with Dr. Benes in Prague on this same subject the President straightened a crooked forefinger: 'That,' he said, 'is what Zionism is doing for the Jew.'

In 1916 he met Chaim Weizmann at breakfast with Lloyd George and was deeply impressed. It was as a result of this new acquaintance that during his war-time visit to America he made it his business to get into touch with American Zionists, from whom he learnt more about the theory and the concrete aspirations of the movement. He also discussed with Colonel House the question of making a National Home for the Jews in Palestine one of the Allies' war aims. On his return to England he kept in touch with Zionist organizations in London and addressed several meetings. Although he was to learn a great deal more about Zionism in later years he already had very clearly in his mind the two strongest reasons for his belief in it.

In this question, as in so many others, his deep belief in the libertarian mission of his countrymen was very marked. For Palestine as for India he envisaged a happy future as a free Dominion of the British Commonwealth, an idea which he elaborated in his book *The Seventh Dominion*. He was naturally also a leading figure in the Seventh Dominion League when that came to be formed in the later 'twenties. It is important to remember how sincere and how firm were his hopes for this solution in the early days of his Zionism. His disappointment and disillusion at the policy of the British government were as great as his hopes had been high.

Until he became closely connected with the Zionist movement he had known chiefly the aristocrats of the intellectual Jewry which had grown up in England in the nineteenth century. Now, meeting Jews of different forbears and backgrounds, he began to understand more fully their complex problems. It was not his way to be uncritical of his friends, his family or

his country. His attitude to the Jews was therefore by
no means one of blind affection. For them, as for all
those he loved, he set up exacting standards. Thus, as
early as July 1918, when the Hebrew University was
being founded in Palestine, he spoke his hopes aloud:

You are going to do something even greater than lay the
foundations of a Hebrew University. You are to lay a
foundation stone to convert a race into a nation — more than
a nation, an inter-nation. You Jews come from all quarters
of the globe. In Palestine you are to set up your own house.
See that it is a home where the evils of all the old nations
will be forgotten; where centuries of intolerance will be
ended in centuries of tolerance. There is a society in this
country which believes the English are the ten lost tribes. In
two respects I believe the Jews and the English resemble
each other. Firstly, both nations can fight for liberty.
Secondly, it is said that we are a nation of shopkeepers;
you are said to be a nation of usurers. Those who know
both nations are aware that both are nations of dreamers
and idealists. Judæa, England and America are the great
homes of idealism and altruism. America is in the war
solely through idealism. See to it that in Palestine you set
up a land of idealism and freedom, not merely a land of
Jews.[1]

He believed also fervently in the virtue of self-help.
To another Zionist audience he said once: 'I have use
for but two words in the Hebrew tongue. Those words
are *Erez Israel*, Stand up and play the man, O Israel.
Turn your Wailing Wall into silicate bricks for your
new factories. Drop the harp for the trumpets which
rang round the walls of Jericho . . . We want more of
the Maccabees and less of Jeremiah.'

Although a Zionist, Josiah never condemned the
non-Zionist Jew any more than he condemned any

[1] *Zionist Review*, July 1918.

other immigrant. He wished to see a new Jewish state but he had no wish to stand in the way of anyone who had the good sense to want to be English or American whatever their race of origin. He felt that newcomers to England were for the twentieth century what French Huguenots or Flemish weavers had been in the fourteenth and seventeenth centuries. While he furthered the cause of Zionism by voice and pen he was far from making adherence to the Zionist creed his condition of friendship to individuals, and he was as willing to help the non-Zionist Jew as the Zionist when it came to the time of persecution.

But he disapproved strongly of the Jew who rejected his people in distress. Once in America an appeal to a wealthy Jew for a subscription was answered by the boast: 'I am a hundred and ten per cent American.' 'Listen,' said Josiah, 'I am an Englishman. I can trace my family quite far back and we have always been just Englishmen. Yet I am only a hundred per cent English. Suppose you content yourself with being a hundred per cent American and give the remaining ten per cent to the Palestine Fund.' He got his subscription.

II

The Balfour Declaration had his wholehearted approval and he watched the development of the post-war situation in Palestine with considerable anxiety. The first serious Arab-Jewish clash occurred in April 1920 when Arab fanatics invaded the Jewish quarters of Jerusalem, killing and looting. Official references to this catastrophe, against which the administration had taken insufficient precautions, described it as the 'disturbances' in Jerusalem. 'Pogrom' was the uglier word on the lips of the Zionists, and Dr. Weizmann in a natural but unwonted burst of rage congratulated Lord Lothian (then Mr. Philip Kerr) on 'the first pogrom under the British flag'.[1]

After the 'disturbances' arrests were made on both sides since some of the Jews had defended themselves. Others, more correctly gauging the temper of the Arab fanatics than the administration had done, had provided themselves with arms. Lieutenant Jabotinsky, who had been chiefly responsible for this precautionary measure, was sentenced to fifteen years imprisonment. Josiah immediately rose in the House of Commons to ask the Prime Minister 'whether Lieutenant Jabotinsky, the man who fought in Gallipoli and afterwards raised the Jewish battalion in London and took them to Palestine, has been sentenced to fifteen years imprisonment for attempting to raise a force in Jerusalem to defend his co-religionists during the recent pogrom; and if so will he have an inquiry made with a view to his release'.

The sentence on Jabotinsky was quashed a few weeks later and the inquiry in Palestine led to the Churchill White Paper of 1922 which re-affirmed the Balfour Declaration, asserted that Arab interests would also be protected and guaranteed immigration of Jews into Palestine in proportion to the economic capacity of the country to absorb them. The energy and labour of the Jews already there was yearly increasing that capacity and in 1922 few Gentiles foresaw the appalling persecutions which were so vastly to swell the number of refugees in the later 'thirties and the 'forties. Yet there were sporadic troubles in

[1] Chaim Weizmann, *Trial and Error*, p. 324.

Eastern Europe and in Poland the advent of the Pil-
sudski dictatorship was celebrated by attacks on the
Jews. This particular phenomenon worried Josiah a
good deal. He believed in self-determination and independence; it could, he thought, only do a people good
to be liberated from oppression and set up as a free
nation. But the Poles were no sooner a free nation
than they turned arrogantly nationalist and set on the
Jews . . . Would the Jews turn out the same way? He
hoped not. The situation of the Jews in Hungary, and
still more in Rumania, filled him with anxiety and he
deplored the attitude of British diplomatists who,
throughout the 'twenties and 'thirties, turned a blind
eye to what was happening in these countries. In
Josiah's view the duty of the British Ambassador or
Minister in a small Balkan state — or indeed in any
state — was to express emphatic moral disapproval of
any uncivilized or oppressive conduct. Great Britain's
part was always and everywhere that of protector of
the distressed. Very bitterly did his country disappoint
him in these years.

In the autumn of 1926 he and his wife went on a
holiday tour — a holiday as he understood it — of the
Eastern Mediterranean. The Akropolis took his
breath away and he liked the political enthusiasm of
the Greeks: 'In the evening the men meet at the local
cafés and discuss politics and the need of leaders.
Greeks always discuss politics, and most believe they
could be leaders.' Of Jerusalem he wrote with less
passion, but he observed and spoke a great deal. He
was particularly struck with the communal farms, and
by the independence, energy and good sense of the
people. In these settlements he saw the realization of
some of his hopes for a new, proud and self-reliant
Judaea. He saw, too, both in the settlements and in

the feeling of the landless Jews, more evidence for Henry George's conviction that free land solves all problems. All the more therefore he deplored the obstacles which the administration now put in the way of Jews trying to take over unused Arab land.

There would be no unemployment in Palestine [he wrote], if the land which is not being used could be made accessible to the men who want to start doing what other more fortunate Jews are doing... Deep in the consciousness of every Jewish worker in Palestine is now the certainty that the land question is at the root of all their difficulties.

On the way back he visited the Sephardic colony at Salonika. Here he addressed an enthusiastic audience in French. 'They said they had never heard anything so Parisian,' he wrote to his daughter, 'and being Levantines of course they know.' He carried away the warmest memories of these Spanish-speaking intellectual aristocrats of Jewry who for many years never failed to send him annual greetings. Of this noble and gifted race very few survived the Second World War.

Eighteen months later he was touring South Germany and Rumania. In Rumania he was received by Queen Marie and Princess Marthe Bibesco, who gave valuable countenance to what the Rumanian government would otherwise have considered outrageous conduct. Jews were not liked under that military despotism and bewildered Army officers would turn up to stare at the eccentric English colonel, the gentile Zionist. Their precarious situation made the Rumanian Jews unduly nervous. At Czernovitz, in a crowded hall, a flashlight photograph caused a moment's panic. Fearing a bomb, the audience flung themselves towards the stairs, which were steep and narrow and made of stone. Josiah called from the platform in German, 'Stop, stupids. All Jews will now sing the Hatikvah.' Obediently they sang and disaster was averted.

III

By this time Zionism had come level with and passed India as Josiah's chief interest outside his own country. The reasons were fairly clear. India had a number of non-Indian champions beside himself. Zionism had few non-Jewish advocates. Although the Indian struggle might be long and hard there was little doubt that Indian independence would be achieved in the end. Everything pointed that way; it was merely a question of when and how. The Zionist cause was on a different footing. Here the difference was not between a longer and a shorter struggle, but between victory and defeat. The forces massed against Zionism both inside and outside Palestine were strong while the mandatory power was weak and undecided, as the renewed riots of 1929 and subsequent events were to show.

In 1930 Josiah and Florence went to South Africa, to enlist further support for the Zionist cause. The journey out was the best part of this disquieting experience. The boat was full of interesting people, including the Prince of Wales, who played the then fashionable game of 'peggitty' with Florence. He was so fond of this pastime that Josiah, with his usual devotion to the Wedgwood business, wrote off at once to his eldest brother Frank to ask whether a 'peggitty' board in solid Wedgwood ware could not be made specially for H.R.H.

The South African visit itself was financially successful but politically depressing. All the heroes of Josiah's youth were either in eclipse or fighting a losing battle for liberalism against the rising forces of race-hatred. He found the opinions of the South African Jews harder to bear. He himself vehemently championed the native and coloured population of South Africa. They bitterly disapproved this attitude. Moreover he was shocked at the support they gave to the bill to prevent further Jewish immigration from Poland and Eastern Europe into the Union. Josiah did not expect all Jews to be Zionist, but found their unwillingness to jeopardize their position undeserving of sympathy. This was the kind of expediency to which he opposed an unrelenting disapproval. Money for Palestine was, however, generously given in response to his and his wife's eloquent appeals, so that the tour, though unhappy, was by no means unsuccessful.

Renewed disturbances had meanwhile occurred in Palestine. There followed in due course the setting up of the Royal Commission, against the composition of which Josiah protested because no member of Parliament was included. He himself was Chairman of the Parliamentary Committee on Palestine.

He fought hard against the policy of J. H. Thomas at the Colonial Office and the suggested constitution for Palestine of 1936. He had always been opposed to the idea of a communal roll for representation which he believed had done great harm both in India and Cyprus. The communal roll in his view created a vested interest in preserving the existence of a minority and perpetuating, or even accentuating, divisions. In his opinion the system of voting should be such as to create solidarity, to emphasize common interests and minimize divisions, while the interests of the minority were protected by the necessity for wooing their support. If all else failed, he even preferred the idea of nominated representatives for minorities, because these at least created no vested interest. He thus saw in the proposed constitution a certain method of perpetuating the Jew-Arab hostility and increasing the violence of fanatic minorities. His opposition to the 1936 Constitution was not in vain. 'I have had a successful week,' he wrote to his daughter Camilla at the end of March, 'actually slain the Palestine Constitution. I got Churchill and Chamberlain and Amery and Sinclair all to speak, and they did, leaving the Rt. Hon. J. H. Dress-shirt in tears.' There was certainly no love lost between Josiah and the Colonial Secretary in those years.

He protested yet more strongly against the proposed partition of 1938. This in particular had the worst possible effect on the situation, since it encouraged the Arab nationalists to further acts of terrorism and increased Jewish distrust of the mandatory power. Jewish para-military organizations were by now coming into existence to resist, or to retaliate against, the Arab gangsterdom which the authorities seemed unable to control. Members of the Jewish organizations were arrested; so were the illegal immigrants who fled before the Nazi menace. Some of them were marched through the streets manacled together under armed guard. To the President of the Jewish Former Army Officers Association who described these things to him, Josiah in May 1938 wrote as follows:

Your letter of May 10th has given me much thought. I know all that you say is correct, but how to improve the situation troubles me. I am afraid that mere asking for justice, or asking *my* help, is useless. In my experience, especially in times of difficulty, governments only give way

to action. Demands backed by nothing but a sense of
justice, play little part in modern history. The Czechs
would be under Nazi rule today if they had not decided to
fight and die. So would the Spaniards. The Arabs — or
those who are troublesome — get their way in Palestine
because they act instead of petition.

I do not think reprisals in the form of murdering
innocent Arabs is morally justifiable. When ordinary law
breaks down lynch law generally takes its place. That is
better than murdering innocent people; but I cannot advocate that, nor can I judge of its necessity. But I think you
are morally entitled to arm to defend yourselves and your
outlying colonies, and to erect such defences as are possible.
This I have no doubt you have done.

There remains such passive resistance as Gandhi put
into practice in South Africa and in India. Such action
needs solidarity and the will to suffer by going to prison. I
think it needs also the social boycott, and the giving up of
normal relations with the governors. You cannot dine *and*
denounce.

Passive resistance takes several forms:

1. The occupation of land and refusal to leave except by
   the force of law, and going to prison;
2. Refusal to pay taxes, breaking the law, and going to
   prison;
3. Refusing to plead in the Courts or to recognize their
   jurisdiction and going to prison;
4. Attending demonstrations which have been declared
   illegal;
5. Distribution of illegal literature;
6. Assisting illegal immigration;
7. Picketting and boycotting the disloyal.

Last year some Jewish illegal immigrants were
marched in chains to Acre gaol. I think if you had freed
them on that march, even by violence, British public opinion
would have supported you, and it would never have occurred
again.

Now Jews are sent to concentration camps or gaol

without trial or charge, and no protest or demonstration is made by the other 450,000 Jews in Palestine. You expect me to protest in Parliament. I am not going to do so any more. It is for the Jews in Palestine to stop that sort of thing. The same applies to Jews arrested for carrying arms. The Bastille was pulled down for less than this. You do not even sit down and strike before the gaol gates when they hunger strike. Naturally they think they can do anything to Jews.

Or to *some* Jews? If there is no solidarity among all Jews; if some Jews go to the government and apologize for other Jews; in that case you will get nowhere. The Trades Unions or Histaduth set you a powerful example. They strike and get their way against Tel Aviv Council, or against the orange growers. Why should the Government be sacrosanct? United you stand, divided you will always fall. You must have a willingness to suffer as well as a united willingness to help the sufferers.

If I were a British official in Palestine, I too should get 'fed up' with your complaints, and should respect you much more if you cursed, and acted in pursuit of justice for your fellow countrymen. You curse 'them' behind their backs; try cursing them to their face — not *you* only, but the Press also. If you dare not, you are not worthy of your country. If you do, and not till then, they will think you worthy of arms to use in defence of the Empire and Democracy.

Like you I want to see a free, manly, fighting people, like the Maccabees, in Palestine once again. I want to see an army of 40,000 Jews fit to defend all that you and I hold dear. With reluctance I have come to the conclusion that only by the hard road laid down above can we arrive.

You have my free permission to show this letter to Mr. Shertok, to the High Commissioner, and to the Commander-in-Chief. All three will agree, but none of them will dare to say so. I know my fellow countrymen a good deal better than you do.

You ask me 'to imagine myself in your place with my own kith and kin attacked and my hands tied'. I can imagine nothing of the sort. An Englishman's hands would *not remain* tied; and yours are only tied by unworthy fear.

I cannot possibly give you any clear idea of what to do anywhere at any time. I can only suggest that when anything unpleasant occurs, consider what action British colonists would take under the circumstances; and if you do about half you will not ever need to do it again.

Josiah had no intention that this letter should be treated as confidential. He intended it to be shown to those in authority. He intended it to circulate among the Jews. Yet he was perhaps a little surprised by the extent to which it was copied, circulated, discussed. It was reproduced in a pamphlet which was distributed in defiance of the mandatory power. The administration made it illegal for any Jew to possess a copy.

His action in writing it was vigorously criticized not only by those opposed to Zionism but by many who had hitherto been his friends. He was felt to have jeopardized the Government's policy of conciliation and to have destroyed the hopes which had been based on the passive acquiescence of the Jews until the situation cleared up. It should be remembered, however, that Jewish feelings had already been exacerbated beyond endurance and the letter owed its popularity and its influence to its exact reflection of their feelings. Defending his action in a letter to *The Times*, Josiah wrote:

> The violence and anarchy today is worse than ever, because the policy of conciliation is still continued, and untrustworthy Arab supernumerary police are armed for no reason save to balance the arming of Jewish supernumeraries. The Administration continues strictly impartial between murderers and murdered ... We who have urged patience on the Jews in hope of a change have no right to do so any longer. (*Times*, July 21st, 1938.)

Whatever the initial rights and wrongs in the Palestine question, there was little doubt by 1938 that the Jews had lost almost all faith in the British Administration which had failed to protect them from attack; its behaviour, as they saw it, conformed closely to Josiah's descriptive phrase of scrupulous impartiality 'between murderers and murdered'.

IV

Meanwhile, in November 1938 the worst pogrom yet experienced began in Germany and the flood of refugees seeking entry to Palestine swelled from day to day. Almost immediately after came the White Paper of 1939 by which the British Government announced its intention of suspending the immigration policy embodied in Mr. Churchill's White Paper of 1922. In future other considerations besides the economic capacity of Palestine would be taken into account in settling the quota, and after a five-year interval no further immigration would be permitted without Arab agreement. This was no less than the calculated closing of one of the few doors of escape left to the terror-stricken millions in Germany and Eastern Europe. Now began the tragic procession of illegal immigrants, the first part of whose story culminated with the disasters of the *Patria* and the *Struma*.

The initial victories of Hitler in the war led to intensified persecutions in Hungary and Rumania and in all occupied countries. The gas chambers of Auschwitz and the unspeakable laboratories of Ravensbruck were already working. Small wonder that overloaded boats, crammed with frantic fugitives, now ploughed the eastern Mediterranean. The British authorities refused permission to land; those who landed were interned and, if possible, subsequently deported. Mauritius was one destination selected for them but it is not surprising that rumours went about that illegal immigrants were being sent back to face the terror; it is not surprising that there were disturbances outside internment camps and on the quays. The passengers on the *Patria* were refused leave to land, whereupon the ship blew up in Haifa harbour and those who survived swam ashore. It never became clear whether the explosion was accidental or a deliberate and desperate attempt to force the British authorities to rescue, and thus to give protection, to the survivors. The shocking story of the *Struma* disaster makes the latter explanation the more probable.

The *Struma*, a yacht which had been reconditioned to carry passengers, set sail from Costanza in December 1941 crammed far above capacity with 750 Jewish refugees of all ages and sexes. The Turkish authorities at Istambul, acting in agreement with the British authorities in Palestine, refused to allow the *Struma* to proceed to Haifa. The passengers refused to go back to Costanza. For thirteen weeks negotiations went on and at the end of that time the British authorities agreed to take the children between eleven and sixteen. It is not known whether this message ever reached the passengers on the *Struma*. About the time when it should have been received, the ship had put out to sea; five miles out, she blew up with all on board.

Josiah's mind and heart were full of the *Struma* disaster when, a few days later, he broadcast to the United States in the following terms:

The chief merit of Dr. Weizmann is that he seeks to restore or create the self-respect of the Jewish people. I think that the creation of self-respect should be the great aim of all

statesmen everywhere ... In Palestine the Jew is on horse-
back, head up, free from the care of what others may think
of him. At home! I used to think that the first step towards
freedom was to get the land. Give me the land and I will
produce the men. In 1942, in a worse world, I must reverse
the order. Give me the men and they can take the land —
only the men must be armed. In 1942 men without arms
don't count, and have no rights. Presently, they have no
food and live no longer. That is why Victor Cazalet and I,
and that handful of God's good Englishmen who still put
duty and conscience above subservience to any government,
have formed a committee to concentrate effective action on
the arming of the Jews. The arguments are mostly obvious.
The more people there are to help us destroy Hitlerism the
better. Not to allow them to fight for their own land and
their skins by our side is inhuman and treachery to all that
we fight for.

These reasons I have given are obvious. Yet why is it
forbidden to arm? Let us be frank. We have nothing to
conceal any longer. Our enemies know already why we
want the Jews of Palestine armed — and why the British
forbid it. We want the Jews of Palestine armed in the sure
and certain conviction that, once armed, they will never
surrender those arms, save with their lives, either to Hitler's
Germans or the British Administration in Palestine. First
arms, then land, then freedom! Yoked for twenty-five years
in double harness the end has come. Twenty-five years of
what should have been co-operation have been twenty-five
years of jealousy, malice and uncharitableness, ending in
the mass massacre of the *Struma*. The British Administration
have been too strong for the British Parliament and conscience. The whole Administration from the top to the Irish
Police who masquerade as British, are against the half-
million Jews of Palestine. They will never let them have
arms, nor land, nor free immigration, nor a refuge, nor a
home — never! They don't like Jews. And there are enough
anti-Semites and crypto-Fascists still in Great Britain to
back up the Hitler policy and spirit.

Some think that it will be all right at the end of the war; that the *Struma* and the *Patria* and the shootings and concentration camps are all forced upon the British Government to prevent the Arabs making trouble just now. Wishful thinking! The Arabs are an excuse, not a reason. Any change now must involve the whole Administration. They have all a vested interest in proving the Balfour Declaration unworkable, in proving themselves right. There is no longer any hope for any British Administration. The bombs that blew up the *Struma* blew too deep a gulf between. It was the logical and inevitable end of a policy. Therefore seek to get your America to act, to press for freedom and justice, to accept the mandate, to build another free land, with open doors and open hearts. I am speaking to you Stephen Wise and to you Hillel Silver. I have tried to save for my own countrymen the glory of rebuilding Jerusalem, of doing justice, of creating freedom. It is no use: they won't do it. I cannot help it. You must turn to America and must take on the job yourselves. Ask no more from Britain. You make yourselves too cheap. You weary us. We prefer King Ibn Saud and King Farouk, and veils and fezzes and the Middle Ages.

I speak also to you, Senator Wagner. You are as devoted to your people as I am to mine. You are as proud of America as I am of England's past. Will you see where lies America's duty? Can you take on the job from our enfeebled hands? The responsibilities of the whole world have lain on our shoulders long enough. It's your turn now. The mantle of Elijah has fallen upon Elisha — not only in Palestine. It is your rendezvous with destiny. And, if it should occur to you to think poorly of the way in which we have acquitted ourselves, if you see too many black pages in our history, reflect that all nations that have ruled have such black pages, but see at the same time in our history, as in America's that at least there have always been men to denounce the crimes of their own Government, to seek to right the wrong. You and I, Senator Wagner or Senator Lodge, we may not succeed, but we can keep our country's name clean by daring to be in the right with two or three. Then some day even the Jews will find justice and respect, perhaps even gratitude. We may all look forward to the day when there will be no leaving it to England, or leaving it to America, when joined in a Federal Union of the Free, the Jews of Palestine may be partners. Then neither isolated America, nor isolated England shall be any longer afraid to do its duty. . . .

This vehement appeal marked a revolution of spirit. He who had believed in the English mission no longer believed in it. He had travelled a long way from the time when he had helped to found the *Seventh Dominion League* to bring Palestine into the Empire. The suggestion made to the United States was the measure of his bitter disillusion with British methods. This was a great blow to him, perhaps the greatest in his life. He believed intensely in the nobility of the English ideal, at its best, and was convinced that, in the long run, British rule was beneficial, as being both just in itself and instructive in the art of democracy. He would have agreed with what his old friend, that great fighter for Indian independence, Lajpat Rai had said:

'British rule in India has its brighter side. Young India has drunk deep from the springs of liberty and the rights of man, as embodied in English history and literature.' He conceived of the British Empire as a great educational power in the world, he believed in it as a force working for justice and democracy. That was why he had striven to convert a British-ruled India into an independent democratic India. That was why he had fought for twenty years against mismanagement in Palestine.

Now, in the second world war, just when he saw his country fighting magnificently on every front to rescue and restore liberty from the Nazi menace, he saw the Palestinian authorities shutting the doors on the victims of Nazi persecution, refusing to allow the Jews to fight beside the other peoples for liberty, and showing, as he thought, unmistakable signs of anti-Semitic prejudice in the internal affairs of Palestine.

The thing was to him infinitely tragic; tragic because of those who suffered in Palestine, because of the *Struma* victims, and the millions caught by the Nazi ferrets in the rabbit warren of Eastern Europe with every earth stopped; but tragic most of all because the great tradition of his country was being betrayed. This was action unworthy of England. Only because he felt this did he make that unsponsored appeal to America. If 'God's Englishmen' failed to live up to the traditions of their past, it was up to God's New Englishmen to take up the burden.

How the cautious B.B.C. came to let through this astonishingly outspoken broadcast remains a mystery. There was trouble for someone, to Josiah's indignation, for why should others suffer for letting him say what he felt must be said. There was also some trouble for him in the House of Lords, but he was used to fighting his Palestinian battle and stood his ground.

Your grievance against me [he said] is not what I said but that I said these things to America and not here from my place in Parliament. Let me explain. The barrier between us and Americans is that we do not speak of them or to them as though they were Englishmen or Scotsmen, but as though they were foreigners — not with perfect frankness, but with the language of diplomacy, as though we have to make a case, to justify our conduct, our past. If we are going to work with them — ultimately, as I hope, to unite with them — all this 'my country right or wrong stuff' simply exasperates, and I believe it is intended to do so. There are many pages in our history of which we are ashamed. So there are in America's. Decent people in Britain and America are not going to conceal them, slur them over, or

defend them. What we can point to, in both countries, is
that every crime of government has found men to denounce
their own Government, and ultimately to convert public
opinion. In that we are almost unique. It is our most
glorious tradition. Chatham denouncing the war with the
Thirteen Colonies; Burke denouncing the pillage of India;
Wilberforce denouncing the slave-trade; Ashley Cooper
denouncing the factory-system; Bright denouncing our
support of the South in the Civil War; Mill denouncing the
crimes of Governor Eyre — we owe something to these men,
all Members of Parliament. We owe just what America
owes to Lloyd Garrison, to Lowell, and to Lincoln, and those
who in recent days defended, even with honour, as the Lord
Chancellor will admit, Sacco and Vanzetti, or the Scotts-
borough negro boys. It is these people who have made our
joint united traditions . . . Why did I appeal directly to
America? Because I am not playing a game, but trying to
get arms for the Jews. Why did I tell the Americans the ugly
truth? Because I wish to force the hands of the British
Foreign Office. It is not enough for our good name to make
empty protest. I want results, not the recitation of a litany.
We followed up the massacre of Amritsar by the dismissal
of General Dyer. We followed up the murder of the Czechs
at Munich by hooting Chamberlain out of office. I hope yet
to live to see those who sent the *Struma's* cargo back to the
Nazis hanged as high as Haman, cheek by jowl with their
prototype and Führer, Adolf Hitler. Do noble Lords think,
even if it was the only way, it was wrong to tell America?
Americans are with us now in the fight against Hitler. How
much longer is the farce to continue of measuring out what it
is wise to tell those who fight and die beside us?

He did not speak on this occasion like a sick and
tired man, but he was both, and dispirited too. Yet
he continued the fight to the end. He had received
evidence, some of it very strong, of the anti-Semitic
prejudice of the Palestine police. To his angry grief he
found that the Colonial Office refused to make any

THE LAST OF THE RADICALS

thorough inquiry into the matter, while every attack —
and he made several — in the House of Lords, was
thrown back in his face from a wall of indignation.
The usual response was to state that the Palestine
police were splendid fellows and not to be criticized.

What does the noble Lord, Lord Morris, say? [protested
Josiah on one of these occasions]. He says those men are an
excellent body of men. That has nothing to do with anti-
Semitism. I can imagine that there are quite a number of
anti-Semites who might be described as an excellent body of
men. I should not so describe them. That does not affect
my views. If you have a police force anywhere holding
political views you are ruining your civilization and your
democracy. You have now growing up all over the world
these police forces of the Gestapo type who are politicians in
uniform interfering with our lives. You have got that, or the
beginning of it, in Palestine, and unless you stop it the danger
will get worse and will finally destroy any chance of
democracy in that country. I am always losing my temper
over this, and I do apologize to your Lordships for doing so.
Here you have a case of twenty-five years of mis-government
— twenty-five years during which the Colonial Office has
not done its duty by that mandated territory, by the people
whom we have put there. I feel that unless some voice is
raised to protest against that we shall be damned in the eyes
of history. Although we have got a black record in the past,
there have always been people who have denounced the
Government at the time for these black pages in history. It
is time that we got rid of the idea that everything is for the
best and that it is a mistake to criticize. Criticism, indeed,
is the secret of good government and you will get more of it.

They did not get much more of it from him for this
was almost the last speech which he made in Parliament. Lord Cranborne had replied with, for him,
unusual bitterness. It was not the opposition of Lord
Cranborne, but a more fell arrest which curbed his

eloquence. His wife, who watched the vehement interchange with Cranborne from the gallery, saw with helpless distress how much difficulty he had in mastering repeated onslaughts of pain during the whole of that afternoon.

The heart trouble had now become too frequent and severe for him to attempt again a speech of any length. 'Both the two last times that I have had to speak,' he wrote to Camilla, 'I have been almost stopped by pain. It spoils oratory.' But he could still summon the strength to ask questions.

He did not live to see the last sorry chapter of British administration, nor the renewed stream of emigrant ships which sailed for Palestine in 1946. One of these vessels was called by his name. In the new state of Israel he is remembered, in the name of a settlement, in the names of streets in new cities. Of the British statesmen who fought, against official opposition, for the establishment of a free and friendly Jewish state, he was perhaps, among Jews, the best known and the best loved. He fought longest, with most tenacity, with most eloquence, and in three continents, that the Jews might stand up once more as a nation among nations. The new state and its leaders will always remember him with gratitude. But far and wide over the four quarters of the globe are scattered those individual Jews who came to him for help in their hour of despair and did not come in vain. For this he will be remembered while their memory lasts, and for his sake and that of others like him the disaster of the *Struma* will count less hard against his countrymen. So long as his name lives among the Jews the honour of his country will be in part redeemed. It is what he would have wanted.

CHAPTER IX

THE LAST OF THE RADICALS

JOSIAH would have attributed many of our succeeding evils to the fatal provisions of the Versailles Treaty. The financial terms caused the European slump which led to the rise of Marxist parties and counter-balancing Fascist repressions. The treatment of Germany prevented the Weimar Republic from establishing itself and thus made way for Hitler.

He did not consider home politics in isolation but always against the wider background of European and world problems. This did not mean that he was indifferent to home problems. His charity, and his sense of political justice, both began at home and of the many hundreds of questions that he asked in the House the majority were concerned with things happening in Great Britain. Besides asking questions in Parliament, he kept ministers and ministries busy with private questions, for his constituents or for those in trouble further afield. Among his letters there is one from Sir Austen Chamberlain, neatly expressing what many ministers must have felt. 'I find your correspondent's statements incredible . . . only I inquire [into it] because you ask me, not because I believe.' Often, no doubt, there were mares' nests, but not always. The incredible does happen.

In his later years the limelight picked him out most often when he was defending Jews or Indians or refugees; this did not mean that they were his only or even his chief interest. Once, in an election address, he had declared that he put North Staffordshire before the whole world; the words could be interpreted in different ways but his native county always had first place in his heart and his constituents knew it.

Of his three best-loved causes, the Single Tax, Zionism and India, the Single Tax always came first. But this cause did not command public attention as the others did, so that his advocacy of it was not much noticed outside the ranks of the faithful. Four times in vain (in 1928, 1929, 1932 and 1933) he tried to introduce a Bill for the Taxation of Land Values. In 1937 he supported a private member's bill for the same purpose, but it was defeated.

In his private actions he lived up to his beliefs. There is, on a road near to his home in Staffordshire, a small and useful monument to his views and principles. His own letter to the authorities responsible gives the story best.

> A year or two ago I bought a piece of land at Peace-haven, near Brighton, and I have recently sold it at a profit of £50 without having done anything to improve the value of the property. As you know I am always protesting against this sort of thing, or rather against the system of rating and taxation which makes it possible. I therefore do not feel entitled to retain this profit. It seems to me, after consulting with Councillor William Campion, that the best use I can make of the money would be to erect a few seats along the new road from Wolstanton to Knutton, on which old people could rest and from whence they could contemplate the increasing land values on the side of a road due to the expenditure of ratepayers' money. Could you accept the cheque for that purpose?

Towards the end, though he maintained the belief, he recognized that, at least for the time being, that battle was lost. Yet, had anyone asked him, as they asked his hero Major General Harrison on his way to the scaffold, 'Where is your good old cause now,' he would have answered with Harrison's words, 'Here, in my bosom.'

Another strictly home issue on which he felt strongly was the alteration of the Prayer Book. He was prepared in lighter moments to make a joke of his rooted anti-Popery convictions, but they were by no means a laughing matter. His family, like many other industrial families, had returned to the Church from nonconformity during the evangelical epoch of the earlier nineteenth century. Anything that looked or smelled 'High' filled him with suspicion and like many other Anglican laymen he viewed the introduction of the Reserved Sacrament as the first step back to Rome.

He did not speak in the great Prayer Book debate of 1927 when the new Book was rejected, as he preferred to leave the floor to those who knew more about the details of doctrine, but he always admitted to having felt the occasion more deeply than anything else between the wars. The Parliamentary correspondent of a Glasgow paper asserted that he shed tears of relief when the Book was defeated; he never denied it and I believe it may well have been true.

Josiah never neglected the needs of his potter constituents. He was particularly concerned for the health and happiness of the boys and girls widely employed in the potteries. He strove to have polycythaemia, the occupational disease of the industry, included in the Workman's Compensation Act of 1925, and did not give up the fight until it was officially recognized as an industrial disease. The borough of Newcastle-under-Lyme held him especially dear for his efforts to prevent its absorption into the County Borough of Stoke-on-Trent. Stoke is the larger and the newer town. Newcastle has gradually become a suburb on the western flank of the great conglomeration of the

Five Towns. (It is not one of them and would scorn to be so considered.) It has an ancient and long pre-industrial history and has sent members to Parliament since the fourteenth century. Its preservation as a separate entity was something that Josiah would have fought for in the interests of history and tradition even if he had had no other reason for so doing. His efforts were successful; the grateful citizens bestowed on him the freedom of the city in 1930 and thereafter he was twice its mayor. It may also fittingly be added here that in the 1935 election, his last, all three parties, Conservative, Labour and Liberal, declared themselves well content to nominate their incorrigible Independent to represent Newcastle in Parliament. Only the secretary of the local Communist party refused to be associated with this unorthodox proceeding.

The year 1930, which saw his local apotheosis as saviour of the borough and mayor, was pleasant to him, in its earlier months at least, for other reasons. It was the bicentenary of the birth of his namesake 'old Josiah' and both the Potteries and the family prepared to mark the occasion with suitable rejoicings. George Bernard Shaw came down to address an enormous throng of potters; there was a pageant and great celebrations at the Works. Josiah as a younger son had not had the chance of entering the family business. It had expanded since his youth and a flourishing American house had been added to it. There was by this time plenty of room for the younger generation, and it was a source of great pride and joy to him that his second son, also Josiah, had recently joined the firm. With even more than his usual zest he therefore sat down to compose an historical account for the occasion. He added — he could not resist it — an imaginary dialogue between himself and the Founder in which old Josiah expressed satisfaction at the news of America's greatness ('Do you mean Franklin's Thirteen Colonies?'), responded with interest to the theories of Charles Darwin, and learned with gratification that there was now a universal franchise which had sent his great great grandson to Westminster. The august shade continued his interrogation:

'What are your politics?'

'Yours sir. Hatred of cruelty, injustice and snobbery, and an undying love of freedom.'

Then I heard a voice say, 'Carry on,' and the Prince of Potters vanished.

The year did not end so happily. Josiah was now fifty-eight years old and living with the reckless expenditure of energy of a young man. He was taken ill while addressing a luncheon of Individualists. Ordered a complete rest, he went away for a cure and it was while he was in a nursing home that his younger brother, Ralph, brought him the unexpected news of the sudden death of their eldest brother Frank. The most genial and generous of men he had set the tone of the family for many years and had taken the place of a father to his younger brothers ever since they were boys. He had by no means always approved of Josiah's politics but his loyalty and affection had never failed. The blow was a heavy one to the whole family and to one of Josiah's deep feelings very hard to bear at such a time.

11

With the extinction of the Weimar Republic in 1933 began the long years of anxiety and shame which

THE LAST OF THE RADICALS

ended only with the war. For a little while Josiah allowed himself to hope that the immediate excesses of the Nazi regime had jolted English public opinion out of pacifism and might even jolt MacDonald — whom he wholly distrusted — into a more intelligible foreign policy. A speech he made in the House of Commons in March 1933 immediately after the rise of Hitler, the Disarmament Conference and Mac-Donald's visit to Mussolini is indicative of what were then his hopes. It is also in some passages prophetic:

It is remarkable what a revolution has come about in public opinion in the last fortnight, and it is noteworthy that during the last ten days, at least, the Prime Minister and the Foreign Secretary have been out of this country, and absent from that psychological contact and change which has come over public opinion . . . A fortnight ago all our bright young things were passing resolutions that they would never again fight for King and country. Now they are muttering that if these German supermen go much further, then 'We shall have to tackle them'. That is a change which has come about, and I think it is a tribute to the humane, generous feeling of this country.

What has taken place in Germany has completely converted a pro-German England into a pro-French England, and that change has not yet been obvious to the Prime Minister [MacDonald]. I feel certain that if he had realized what we have been feeling, he would have made in his speech some general reference to his friends who are now hunted from refuge to refuge, from one prison to another — Otto Wels whom we both knew as a Socialist of the bolder type, Dr. Breitscheid the austere, Von Gerlach who had the superb courage all through the war to publish week by week in Berlin *Die Welt am Montag*. All these people are now being hunted and bludgeoned like rats. I would wish that the Prime Minister had remembered that in his speech, and had indicated, as no one but a Prime Minister can indicate, the

210

decent opinion of British gentlemen about the sort of thing going on in Germany. . . .

It is curious the way in which the old, ancient, popular objection to a British Prime Minister going abroad is being revived in this twentieth century. He goes away, and we do not know what he gives away. We do not know what the bargain is that is being struck, and it is exceptionally difficult to discover when he comes back what has been struck. . . .

So far as the Disarmament Conference is concerned, I think the Prime Minister did absolutely right. In his putting forward our case for disarmament he is right, whether season-able or not. He was whisked away from Geneva to Rome to a meeting with that dangerous siren Il Duce Mussolini, and he has never met him before. There were certain little objections connected with the death of Matteotti which made it difficult to effect a meeting before. Now it has happened, and we have seen all sorts of prognostications in the Press as to what was the great plan that Mussolini passed off, almost on the first moment of the first interview, upon the Prime Minister and the Secretary of State for Foreign Affairs, which met so heartily with their approval. It was the revi-sion of the Peace Treaties, and all of us in this House have always been in favour of the revision of the peace treaties. . . .

But when Signor Mussolini thinks of revising the peace treaties, he is thinking before all of the Italian grievances. Under the Treaty of London, I think, framed during the war, when we had to do everything to get allies in the war, rash promises were made to Italy that could not be carried out at the end of the war, because we had not enough spoils to divide; and, when Italy considers a revision of the peace treaties, she thinks of an extension of her control of raw materials and human beings in Africa . . . I should object, and I think every liberal-minded man will object, to handing over the natives of Africa either to the Nazis of Germany, or to the Fascists of Italy. The Italians are not beloved in the Eastern Mediterranean — their rule is an inexperienced rule — and I would ask the Government to think, not merely of British interests, but of native interests as well, before any

change to the detriment of the natives themselves is made in
Tanganyika, or the Cameroons, or any part of Africa or of
the black world where we at present are responsible for the
natives' well-being. . . .

Already he saw clearly that there was no friendship
to be had with dictators at any price which an Englishman should be willing to pay, and no permanent peace
to be had at any price at all. Within a surprisingly
short time he had established himself as the most frequent and outspoken critic of Hitler in the House, a
distinction which had a depressing effect on the sale
of Wedgwood china in Germany. The Works was
rather proud of this. When the plebiscite of May 1933
was held in Danzig he prophesied the course of events
with considerable accuracy.

We know what the result of these elections will be [he said],
but I wonder if the right honourable Gentleman the Foreign
Secretary knows what action he will take when Poland
invokes the League of Nations to restore Danzig to the League
authority, and to remove Hitler. The difficulty is, in all
these problems, that you have to make up your mind some
time or another. If you let Danzig go, what about the
Corridor? Remember the Anschluss; remember Posen.
Nothing worth fighting about, all little things. Schleswig-
Holstein, Alsace-Lorraine.

The only chance of preventing these things happening is
to take a firm line at first and never to give way to weakness.
If you do that, you encourage force . . . Do not let us re-
write the old history of the end of the Roman Empire,
continually buying off hordes by concessions to people
whose appetite you merely whet by your conciliation . . .
We must stand together and not have divided opinions on
when to put our foot down, but realize before the demands
are made that they will be made, and that either we have to
fight Germany now or allow Germany to fight us later on.

When he attempted to bring in a resolution in

defence of democracy MacDonald would not allow it
to be discussed. The resolution ran as follows:

That in the opinion of this House, those democratic
institutions which we have built up, have been and must
remain the sole foundation of ordered progress, of just
prosperity and of liberty; and that this House deplores the
destruction of parallel institutions on the Continent of
Europe, and reaffirms its intention to protect and preserve
the free sovereign Parliament of England.

It was cogently phrased. Had it been put before the
House every member would have been faced with a
difficult choice: either to admit a feeble belief in Parliamentary government or to be offensive to Hitler at a
moment when the Government had decided to be
pleasant to him.

Josiah was an angry man, and rightly angry. His
mail was full every morning of anguished letters from
Social Democrats and Jews trying to escape before the
trap closed. Speaking in the House only a few weeks
after the Nazi revolution, he made the first of his many
appeals for a policy of unrestricted hospitality to the
victims of oppression.

I wish to say one or two words on what has gone on in
Germany. The corner boys of Germany have disgraced
their country and in the language of Italy I would say:
Non ragionam di lor ma guarda e passa. (Hon. Members:
'translate!') It means: 'You need not talk about those people
but watch them for what they are and pass by on the other
side.' As a result of what has gone on in Germany, I would
like to see the strengthening of this country and of the British
race by the admission freely into this country of those
elements which are now suffering from persecution. The
Hon. and gallant Member for Chippenham (Captain
Cazalet) who has just spoken is a Huguenot of distinguished
Huguenot ancestry. Does not everybody today realize the

enormous strengthening of the Anglo-Saxon race that has come from the admission of those Huguenot migrants to this country? They were flying from a persecution that was, I suppose, as bad as that which reigns in Germany today. The dragonnades of Louis XIV sent to this country an element of religion and of independence, and a commercial and intellectual element which has been of inestimable service to this country in war and in peace. I would beg the Government not to miss this opportunity of so benefiting England today and in the future. There we have, driven out of Germany, flying, when they can fly, to all the neighbouring countries, the thinkers, the intellectually independent people, scientists, doctors, civil servants, artists and musicians.

. . . All those people are asking for a home. I wish we had the Home Secretary present. Today those people are being turned back at Harwich, while nations like France, Belgium, Spain — rejuvenated Spain — are welcoming this new intellectual element. Those scientists would be our business men of the future, just as the Huguenots brought us the silk, made Norwich and made Leek in my own county of Staffordshire. The Huguenot element built up a great export trade for this country. We are now anxious to import foreign capital into this country; how much better it is to import foreign brains and amalgamate them. I do not speak from the obvious humanitarian point of view, but from the point of view of the material advantage of this country. Get those people in.

The House will remember that at the beginning of the war we threw our homes open in this country to the people who were flying from Belgium. That was one of the finest effects of the early enthusiasm for our cause. It was humane, and it was also materially advantageous. They produced munitions and helped us in the war. We showed a great sign of international friendship. I wish today that we could do the same. Do not leave it to the Jews. Let English people see whether they, too, cannot receive these people into their family to make a home here, and to show that whatever the Prussian Aryan may feel about the Jews, or the peacemongers or even the Socialists, we in this country realize the value of brains and the duty of hospitality to the oppressed. The position at the present time is almost humiliating for an Englishman. Those people are welcomed in every country, but here nothing is being done. Speeches are made in this House and the subject is given a good run in the Press of all parties, but still the door remains closed. I wish that one result of this Debate today might be the opening of those doors, and the welcoming here not merely of the scientists who make the trade of the future, not merely of the doctors whom in the past all the world has gone to seek in Germany but of those political exiles about whose fates we hear less and who are now under preventive arrest in a dozen concentration camps throughout Germany. I wish that we might welcome those men, the free spirits of a free people, who decline to live in a land where liberty is no longer allowed, and get them here to strengthen our home and our love of liberty.

Appeals reached him daily from the oppressed of Germany. One story is typical. Some years before, while travelling back from Germany, he had fallen into conversation with a Herr and Frau Neumann in a railway carriage. Within a few minutes the friendly Englishman was announcing, 'Meine Familie waren Topfer-meister für drei hundert Jahre in England.' German scholars will perceive that the statement is comprehensible rather than idiomatic. For the benefit of non-German scholars I should perhaps add that it means, 'My family have been potters for three hundred years in England.' The Neumanns to his delight responded at once: 'Then your name is Wedgwood.' Conversation went blithely forward from that happy opening. He told them he had been touring southern Europe; he told them about his children and grandchildren. As they parted he gave them his card, 'if ever you need any help, just send it along'. Why should they need him? A little mystified and a little amused by this generous but unnecessary gesture — as though British M.P.s were a source of strength to all the world — they parted. 'How much we did need it,' writes Frau Neumann. Five years later they were refugees. 'We shall not forget him.'

The story, which I owe to Frau Neumann, is only one of many similar stories. He would uphold the ancient tradition of England as a refuge for the persecuted if he had to do it alone, if he had to do it in the teeth of the Government. He was not alone, for the Jewish community came to the help of its own people, and the Quakers rose to the occasion, as always, for Jews and non-Jews, for all victims of human cruelty. So did many other individuals and institutions. But he was, with many others equally devoted, working against continuous obstruction and misunderstanding. His work as Chairman of the German Refugee Hospitality Committee, which he had helped to form, brought him once more into close contact with many old friends of his youth, as the traditional forces of old Liberalism (the descendants of the Puritans) gathered together to maintain the tradition of English freedom and hospitality. He saw a great deal of the Buxtons in these days, Lord Noel Buxton, Charles Buxton, and his devoted wife, who were throwing everything into the cause of the distressed. He came together again with that great-hearted historian and scholar Dr. Gooch who had entered Parliament with him in 1906 but since withdrawn again to a life of study, and whose house was also now a refuge for the fugitives.

'I write ten letters a day regularly on refugees, the most terrible cases,' he wrote to his daughter Camilla, 'and nothing is done. Last week-end I did fifty. One wouldn't mind if it was any good.' He signed the guarantees which enabled the persecuted to get their pitiful 'transit visas' for England while waiting for the American or the Palestinian quota. The signature was an undertaking to support the refugee during his whole residence in England. He signed so many that the Home Office finally refused to take any more from him and he had to marshal his friends to help. He gave support to many of these exiles in the expansible bedroom accommodation of the Ark. The number of those he saved was about seventy-five: there were hundreds more whom he partly or indirectly helped.

In those years people who came to him for advice were expected to stand on their own feet. I turned up expecting him to help with German friends seeking to escape. He told me whom to get hold of at the Home Office and what to say to him, and sent me off to look after my friends myself. Some people have a gift for getting things done; others, of whom I am one, lack the persistence and the confidence, always lose their place in the queue, fail to make the right impression, wait two hours, three hours, eight hours, two days even — on one occasion — before getting to the right desk in the bureaucracy. But thrown into this sea of conflicting regulations, private goodwill, official obstruction, indifference and anguish, I had to sink or swim, and since on my swimming depended the security and possibly the lives of others, I swam. Neither my experience nor my very minor intervention is worth record in itself, but there must have been many others whom Josiah compelled to do their own fighting, because he could not take on all the fighting himself. Once you had spoken about it to him at all, it was impossible to prove unequal to what he regarded as a duty. Thus recruits were made to the cause of humanity.

He had other things besides Hitler and the refugees on his mind during the 'thirties. There was his visit to Palestine with his wife at the end of 1933. Writing to Camilla in Australia, he announced that he was looking forward to the bathing: 'I shall of course combine it with lecturing the governor and interviewing the oppressed. *Victrix causa deis placuit sed victa Catoni*, which means 'God is on the side of the big battalions but Wedgwoods stand by those who are down'. His anxiety for the future of Palestine and distress that it was not more widely opened to refugees from oppression I have described in a previous chapter.

The granting of a constitution to Russia cheered him slightly about the future of a country in which he had not yet ceased to hope. In an interesting passage in one of his books he declared as late as 1942 his belief that Stalin would ultimately establish a true democracy. The Marshal, he hoped, would not be blind to the object lessons of Roman history and would note that the Antonines had been followed by Commodus. It was his attractive habit to assume in others the familiarity with Gibbon which had formed so many of his own opinions.

On the occasion of the granting of the Russian constitution he was asked, with Lloyd George, to lunch at the Soviet embassy; according to him, Lloyd George raised his glass to the U.S.S.R. and he capped the toast with 'and may they soon be free'.

Inside and outside Parliament he was in perpetual demand as the righter of individual wrongs although sometimes he seems to have been fairly puzzled by the eccentricities of those he defended. Thus he wrote to one of them·

Whenever you get into gaol you write to me, a good habit which reconciles me to your incarceration. Whenever you get out, you not only denounce me as an obsolete old duffer, but send me the denunciatory newspaper and seduce me into reading it. This is a thoroughly bad habit. But what worries me is — Are you an anarchist or a Communist? If the latter, the police may club you and your fellow Communists may save you. If you are an anarchist (colour immaterial), I will put a question and stand by a pal — so long as you tell me what exactly to complain about, i.e. draft the question. If you cannot make up your mind what you are, change your mind.

The British government, meanwhile, with an unshakable majority went on its appeasing way and he raged impotently. The Abyssinian betrayal and the long drawn out farce of non-intervention in Spain followed. At the same time he was fighting his battle with the historians with only Professor Pollard for ally. He wrote to Camilla: 'I am back at work fighting Papists, Fascists and historians. I am becoming speechless over Spain, Palestine, Irak and Germany. Everybody is very kind to me and pays not the slightest attention. Pollard and I have sworn alliance because we are both so old and helpless.' He was, however, neither speechless in the House nor helpless when it came to embarrassing the Government or rescuing fugitives. He still relished battle: 'I do enjoy hitting back at the historians, at traitors, at catholics, at liars, at anybody, even at my age . . . I can't take life seriously even at sixty-six, at least, not all the time,' he wrote.

The Abdication provided a new battle for him, but he was on the losing side. Afterwards he thought he might have been wrong, but his reasons were human and chivalrous. He had never really forgotten the pack of the self-righteous who had set on him over his own divorce, and to him Archbishop Lang appeared suddenly in the guise of Mr. Sinker writ large. Although he got in a phrase of romantic history about 'the King over the water' he was excluded from the abdication debate. Baldwin, whom he always liked, put his arm round his shoulder afterwards with, 'You mustn't mind, Josh. We thought we ought not to allow you to get angry.' Perhaps in the end he did not mind very much, for a few days later he was already re-considering the situation. He received too many letters of congratulation on his words from crypto-Fascists and others whose politics he abhorred. Seven hundred cumbered his desk in the days following; it was the largest fan-mail he had ever had, but 'I have become a hero in strange quarters,' he reflected as he read some of them. As he afterwards wrote to Camilla, 'It was really because I liked him and hated the Archbishop.'

IV

A few months later his young cousin John Cornford was killed fighting in Spain. 'He died fighting and in a good cause, which is not a bad curtain,' wrote Josiah to his eldest daughter, 'I wish there were more of them.' His increasing pride in the younger generation and his confidence in them was certainly one of his most endearing and unusual characteristics. No one ever heard him say that everything and everyone had been better in his young days, and he praised their resilience and sense of adventure in amusing and original terms in his *Testament to Democracy*.

Reflection leads me to the queer conclusion that of all inventions of my age the three of greatest utility have been —

bicycles, Boy Scouts and the cinema, and these because they are valuable as aids to education. All are of great service — playing their different roles in the fit and proper education of the people. Bicycles encourage individual enterprise and self-reliance. Boy Scouts teach self-discipline, courage and unselfishness. Cinemas give vision and imagination. All help to convert dumb, dull, stupid resentful cattle into men fit for self-government and able to use democracy.

He saw the younger generation as a great improvement on the past; braver, more independent, more assured and more sensible.

Another change that gave him pleasure was the revolution wrought in women's clothes by the mass production of ready-made dresses and cheap materials. If the working-class girl in her best can feel that she looks as good as a countess (and indeed *can* so look to the average uncritical male observer) her self-esteem is increased and with it her strength of character. He approved of feminine vanity, in moderation and was glad that, at least in this frivolous respect, human happiness had increased.

His hopes for his own family were always straightforward and straightforwardly expressed. When his eldest granddaughter sent him a handkerchief she had hemmed he thanked her with, 'I say to myself that having made handkerchiefs for a rebel she will never make slippers for a curate.' The same grandchild was taken with a party of younger relations on a trip to the south of France. He approved of early marriages and of letting young people go their own way, but he confessed to qualms on seeing her in close conversation with a young man of Right wing views who was 'something in oil'. But all was well: she was only converting him to sounder opinions on Spain.

This is, however, to leave out a generation. Ethel

had left the children with him when she disappeared in 1913. The five eldest were grown up by the end of the war. Soon after the divorce Ethel went abroad taking her two youngest children, both daughters, with her. All communication with these two children was now virtually at an end. His letters remained unanswered and he was not allowed to see them when he passed through Switzerland and tried to arrange a meeting. Among his correspondence I have found a birthday letter to Julia, the elder girl. I do not know if it was either sent or received. It tells its own story.

Dear little girl,

This is to catch you and give you good wishes on your fourteenth birthday. I have not written to you for so long because I thought you disapproved of me, that for that reason you never replied to my letters; and I was too proud and you too young for any explanation. You are still too young to understand all, but when you grow up you will discover that neither I nor your mother have done anything that we are ashamed of or that need make you ashamed of me. Your parentage is good enough for any child to be proud of. In any case, whether you think hardly of me or not, I love you and I cannot go on for ever hearing nothing of or from you, and for ever wondering if I shall see again my two youngest children.

I wish I knew what you were doing. Do you talk German naturally yet? What are you keen on? Music? or drawing? or dancing? Do you go great walks and expeditions in the Alps? Do you read much? and what? Do you sulk, or explode? or are you contented and smiling? Are you a rebel or a cabbage? Have you acquired wisdom from Goethe's *Faust* or stuff to spout from Schiller's *Glocke*? Do you believe in God or merely in goodness? Do you find it easy or hard to tell the truth? What is the worst vice and what the greatest virtue?

As I lie in bed and write this I only think that, alas, I do not know you at all and cannot help.

Four years later he discovered that she was studying at Stuttgart and, having business in Germany, decided to call on her. He found her among a group of student friends. She was eighteen and he had not seen her for ten years. She was shy, well mannered, not at all sure what to make of a father whom she did not, at first sight, recognize, and deeply loyal to her mother. Later he described her, not without admiration, to one of his elder daughters:

> Magnificent auburn hair brushed straight back à la mamman combined with black eyebrows and eyes the size of saucers ... straight nose, good chin, but the lower lip firm and tight ... So far as I can see none of these young people laugh. Earnestness is the keynote, chiefly about educating themselves or somebody else. When she opened the door to me she gave me the most perfect automatic curtsy that ever Charlotte did to Werther (if she did); *bescheiden* is the word. She is surrounded with a court of young friends (both sexes thanks be), who gaze upwards from a kneeling circle ... Of course like you she is frantically keen on something. In her case it is eurhythmics and the dramatic art. Her whole face lighted up as she talked, beautifully.

Another adventure of the same kind took place a few years later in Vienna when he called on the youngest of his children who had been sent there to study music. 'I have found my secret daughter Gloria,' he wrote to his eldest daughter Helen, 'a pretty dear of eighteen as poor as a church mouse.' Feeling rather like a Knight errant, he took her out and gave her a good time. A little later she came to live with him in England.

His attitude to his children was affectionate, unpossessive, a little erratic. Some of them undoubtedly puzzled him. His eldest son and youngest daughter had talents which were outside his understanding, if not his sympathy, his son being a gifted painter whose career has been hampered by illness, the result of his experiences in the first world war. Gloria, the youngest, was a musician and a 'cellist of some promise until she married and became a mother; this was a profession of which her father approved whole-heartedly. In parenthesis it should be added that he believed in the equality of the sexes, but, since most of the women of his family enjoyed robust health and astonishing vigour, he never really understood why a woman should not rear seven or eight children and do public work as well. Ethel had done so; and so, to his great pleasure, did his eldest daughter Helen, who married the son of the founder of the Fabian Society, and was one of the earliest women J.P.s.

I am so glad our descendants have decided to marry [wrote Josiah to the bridegroom's father, his old friend Edward Pease]. Nothing could have pleased me better — good stock, good brains and good ideals. I do not forget that I came to you — a boy of twenty — to get my first dose of political work; and I like to think that our joint stock will go on with the same work.

His second daughter, Rosamund, whose adventurous journey to Revolutionary Hungary has already been described, subsequently settled in England with her husband. The third, the war-born Camilla, became a distinguished anthropologist and principal of a college in Sydney.[1] The fourth, Julia, has remained in single-minded devotion with her mother. His younger son

[1] His long letters to her across the globe have been an invaluable additional source for his opinions.

Josiah became Chairman of Josiah Wedgwood & Sons, which, of course, was just as it should be.

Josiah's family feeling did not stop short at his own children and grandchildren. All the younger generation of the family interested him; he thought them all splendid and was only distressed when they failed immediately to get married, if possible inside the family itself, and multiply the breed. My brother won approval by marrying his second cousin.

Family pride and political disapproval were at war with each other in his regard for me. We had many common interests, history above all. But then, just when the Government was going from bad to worse and Hitler was in his second year of power, I inadvertently disgraced myself by publishing my first book, a life of Strafford. Strafford to Josiah was a blackbrowed tyrant who had aided and abetted King Charles I in trying to get the better of Parliament; he was incontrovertibly on the Wrong Side. I argued in vain that Strafford, as I then most fervently believed, was an early Socialist and the true originator of the Welfare State. My quondam parlour-pink version of the seventeenth century found no belief with him and would not have helped matters, since State-controlled, State-conditioned, State-compelled happiness was anathema to him, whether it called itself Socialism or National Socialism. He announced in the friendliest way imaginable to all our acquaintances that I had 'blotted the family scutcheon, written a Tory book'. The situation was not improved by the kind Tory reviewers who patted me approvingly on the head in the Press, one of them going so far as to say that this kind of book was a lesson to those ignorant doctrinaires who refused to see the virtues of our modern dictators. We never got the Strafford question straightened out, but

I redeemed myself later by writing some strongly Parliamentarian articles on the tercentenary of the Great Civil War.

He followed the family tradition of unquestioning generosity to less fortunate relations and had the rare gift of being able to bestow charity as though it were a right and a pleasure. Among his letters one, to a maiden-lady whom he wished to rescue from a situation as 'companion', is a model of graceful giving. The offer is made on his own and his wife's part:

My dear Polly,

I hope you won't turn up your nose and turn down our proposition. By accepting this 'dole' you will be giving us much more pleasure than you will give yourself. And I may add that no one in the world deserves freedom more than you do.

I shall expect a return of course — teas whenever I call, 1 lb of honey at Christmas, and the liberties of a relation-in-law whose regard for law is limited.

So tell Miss Amy you are leaving a month from now in order to become a lady — a lady being a person who does not work and is worked for.

v

During the frustrating 'thirties he turned to his work on history and to his family affections for relief from a political situation which he found increasingly bitter. In Parliament and out of Parliament he spoke with more and more vehemence against the policy of the Government, foretelling war with considerable accuracy of detail and urging a wiser armaments policy to meet it. He was one of the few on the Left who did not couple disapproval of Government appeasement with an unrealistic condemnation of rearmament.

Repeatedly, and wisely as it turned out, he urged the necessity of a stronger Air Force and condemned our fumbling defence policy.

A visit to America somewhat raised his spirits, although the sight of the Jewish refugees on the boat filled him with grief at the thought of those whom he was powerless to save. A half-caste singer was eating at a table by herself, so he dined with her every evening. In Washington, 'that superb capital,' he 'worshipped at the shrine of Lincoln, like a marble cathedral with just Lincoln sitting flanked by his speeches, most impressive, more so than the Sistine Madonna'. For once his top measurement of artistic perfection had been surpassed.

He returned in good heart for the struggle in England.

> I am back hard at work [he wrote to Camilla], as well hated by Irish and catholics and historians as ever, and, I can only hope, as well loved by Liberals, rebels and victims. I hate fighting but I have to go on doing it. It is the curse with which I was born ... Here I am after thirty-three years in Parliament, having been everywhere, seen everything, known everybody, done everything — and achieved nothing. The whole world is infinitely worse than it was thirty-three years ago. But if I started again it would all be the same.

The foreign policy of the Government over Spain and Abyssinia and the continued friendliness shown to dictators roused him to an indignant protest. The immediate cause was an article by Scrutator in the *Sunday Times* to which paper he wrote:

Sir,
    The Lord Chancellor writes to tell me that I am intolerant. Lord Macmillan, whom I admire so much (for I once converted him to the taxation of land values), tells

THE LAST OF THE RADICALS

the whole British people the virtues of toleration. And now 'Scrutator' writes an article on the same theme.

'Britons! Mind your own business!' is the Mosley slogan. We who smashed the slave trade and freed the slaves are now to be tolerant and put expediency before justice. Gladstone, denouncing King Bomba's Neapolitan prisons, or Bulgarian and Armenian atrocities, was immorally intolerant. Palmerston, jeering at Marshal Haynau's Austria and welcoming Kossuth, should have held his tongue. Let pogroms in Poland go; let Scottsboro flourish; silence about Dreyfus and Ferrer, about Matteotti and concentration camps. 'Judgment Day' should be banned by the censor. It is not safe — let us be tolerant!

Parliament stopped the Tsar coming to England before the war, and Mannerheim since. Now we are to welcome Goering and make a 'gentleman's' agreement with Mussolini by sacrificing Abyssinia and dropping the mandate for Palestine. We are to tolerate cruelty, injustice and tyranny, as long as it is abroad, because it is wrong to be intolerant and safer to be quiet.

The Catholic Archbishop of Westminster dares to speak of the Spanish insurrection as a crusade. May we not dare to speak of it as a crusade against the poor? Must the Deans of Canterbury and of Chichester be silent on their faith? Must Liberals be silent on their faith, when attacked, because it is wrong to be intolerant? Or because it is unsafe to speak the truth?

It is not unsafe. Our position was won in the nineteenth century, for we secured the respect of the world by standing up to evil and taking the risks like men. Now we are losing that respect, and so losing our strength and our friends. Nor is it even virtuous to condone tyranny and to be silent about wrongs done to others. Pray tolerate my view that we should not even tolerate error. Toleration is the vice of the old, but I hope to die still utterly intolerant, for I am quite sure that the toleration preached today is cowardice. Still, whosoever would seek to save his life shall lose it!

An unpublished letter, which appears to have been intended as a part of this same correspondence, is worth quoting here also, partly because it sums up very well his feelings about the meaning of tolerance and the different responsibilities, in this respect, of the State and the individual.

> You are right in thinking me intolerant and I shall remain intolerant — of cruelty, injustice and error. Toleration in the individual is apt to be another word for laziness and cowardice. The State and the Church should *not* be intolerant because they have the power, they can dictate and enforce conformity. But if the individual 'resists not evil', bows down to power and authority, and washes his hands like Pilate 'innocent of the blood of this just man', then only tyrants prosper while civilization and humanity decay.

Shortly after this correspondence the B.B.C. rather surprisingly invited him to take part in a debate on pacifism. They had intended the debate to be theoretical. But he had no use for theoretical argument when Rome was burning. In his script he flatly asked his opponent what good he thought the appeasement policy would do.

> Concessions to threats and violence do not lead to peace. Even if we could so placate the greater dictators, the lesser dictators might demand similar justice. Franco would then demand Gibraltar and justice; Egypt, the Sudan and justice; Poland might demand Palestine; Pirow may demand Bechuanaland; de Valera might want Ulster first and Liverpool next. Buying off the barbarians might be easier than buying off the dictators ... What Hitler wants is Austria, Czecho-Slovakia, Lithuania, some of Poland and the Ukraine, and I hope the Southern Tyrol — not to mention Switzerland, Alsace Lorraine, Schleswig-Holstein and Malmedy; Mussolini is more moderate, but requires Majorca,

Malta, Cilicia, Palestine, Egypt, Arabia, Tunis and the control of Spain. That is their idea of justice.

The B.B.C. refused to let him say these things and the talk was cancelled. He printed it in full. Between the time at which he wrote and the publication of the pamphlet Hitler fulfilled part of his prophecy by marching into Austria.

Now his attention was fixed with renewed anguish on the tragic problem of the refugees. He tried to introduce a bill for the temporary suspension of the Aliens Acts and Naturalization Acts in favour of the fugitives from persecution. It was in vain. Permission to introduce his Austrian Refugees Immigration Bill was refused by 210 votes to 141.

Events were moving fast towards the Munich crisis, the bitterest moment of his life for he felt his country to be utterly disgraced. Yet in the House on that occasion he kept his deeper feelings remarkably well under control and marshalled arguments based on military and economic considerations against the Chamberlain policy. He pointed out that the Four Power Pact with a subservient Italy and a weak France, meant only an alliance under Germany, an extended Reich. 'The Four Power Pact as it is envisaged and as it is promised by Herr Hitler, is indeed another name for the German Reich.' He showed how economic treaties were almost daily increasing the number of Germany's satellites in Europe and in Latin America. He insisted that the antithesis of opinion was not, as was then widely believed, between those who wanted war and those who wanted peace. This was an essentially false antithesis, because in fact few have ever wanted war. The antithesis was between those who trusted Hitler's word and thought peace could be built on it, and those who did not.

The Right Hon. Gentleman, the Prime Minister is one of those who trust the German Führer. His trust in him has been completed because the German Führer has said that his territorial ambitions in Europe are now satisfied. It was about forty years ago that the father of our present Prime Minister said that he who sups with the devil needs a long spoon, and I regret to have to inform the House that the gentleman referred to in that case as the devil was the German Emperor. If it needed a long spoon then, I am afraid it needs a longer one now; and when I see him being approached by our Prime Minister with a loving-cup, or a loving-trough, into which they may all dip their gas masks together, I ask is this new generation of the Chamberlain family really as reliable as the past? I begin to think we should examine with extreme caution the position into which the Prime Minister is leading this country. . . .

Our quarrel, essentially, is one that is based on the danger arising to this country, and to democracy everywhere, by the unrestricted advance of Hitlerism, and it is against that that we have to prepare ourselves. I would merely point out, to show how we must mistrust the German Chancellor, that even this last stipulation he has made, that all his territorial demands in Europe are satisfied, is merely a remark in conversation between him and the Prime Minister and has not been put on paper — it is not even the 'scrap of paper' which we saw dealt with in 1914. Those who are anxious for the survival in this world, of justice, freedom and democracy trust the German Chancellor less than ever, and quite frankly we regard those who do trust him as fools or traitors to the cause of democracy.

He detested the gas mask distribution and the elaborate but vague defence preparations that went on in those months. 'You must be as well aware as I am,' he wrote to his eldest daughter, 'that gas masks and A.R.P. were solely invented by the Government in order to terrify the old women of this country into welcoming our strong silent Prime Minister on his

return from supping with the devil.' The Houses of
Parliament were suddenly filled with workmen putting
up steel doors for protection against fire and flood. He
smacked one hard as we strolled out of the dining-room
one day, 'Making the place into a bloody bolt-hole,'
he said, using, for him, a most unusual adjective.
'But Uncle Jos,' I said, 'what are you going to do when
the war starts? Go out into the street and breathe in
great invigorating draughts of poison gas?' He gave
me his most enchanting smile. 'There won't be any
poison gas,' he said. He was right.

When war was declared and the sirens wailed out
into the clear blue Sunday morning he offered very
loudly to lay five pounds that there would be no
bombs on London for six months. He won that bet.
During the stunned first week of the war it made first,
surprisingly, headline news, then gossip-column
chatter. He had intended it to serve a purpose — that
of steadying public morale, shaken as he believed it
to be by exaggerated fears. It certainly did its part
in restoring sanity.

If it could not or should not be said that the war
gave him happiness, it gave to him and to many like
him a sense of release. The long frustration was over;
the powers of evil had at last been challenged. For
him, above all, his country had at last proved worthy
of her past. The B.B.C. relented and let him speak
several times in the postscripts after the news, until he
caused official consternation over Palestine as has been
related in a previous chapter.

But he still resented the timorousness of the Government. The atmosphere was wrong. It was he, perhaps
more than anyone else, who stirred up his fellow
members to resist the plan for the evacuation of
Parliament. He was sure, and rightly sure, that for

Parliament to leave London would be psychologically wrong and morally wrong, too.

He has described his feelings during the great debate which ended the Prime Ministership of Neville Chamberlain too eloquently in his own *Memoirs* for me to attempt it again. He had complete confidence in Churchill and, in spite of much disagreement, the warmest admiration that I believe he ever had for any man. He wrote to him soon after he became Prime Minister on the subject which then most disturbed him — the effective defence of England and especially of London. Just as he had been strong in his opposition to any plan for Parliament leaving London, he was strong in his conviction that London and England could be defended against invasion, and that all talk of carrying on the war from Canada should the German invasion of England become a fact was harmful and defeatist.

In July 1940 he put down on paper a scheme for the street by street defence of London and sent it to the Prime Minister.

Many thanks for your letter [wrote Churchill], I am hoping to get a great many more rifles very soon and to continue the process of arming the Home Guard. You may rest assured that we should fight every street of London and its suburbs. It would devour an invading army, assuming one ever got so far. We hope, however, to drown the bulk of them in the salt sea.

The letter itself the Prime Minister forwarded to General Ismay with a note:

See the letter from Mr. Wedgwood, M.P. which is interesting and characteristic. What is the position about London? I have a very clear view that we should fight every inch of it and that it would devour quite a large invading army.[1]

[1] See WINSTON CHURCHILL, *Their Finest Hour*, pp. 235, 571.

He sent another copy to the Secretary of State for War with the note, 'You might do something for Jos. He is a grand-hearted man.'

That autumn Josiah's *Memoirs*, written hurriedly in the preceding year to take his mind off the anxieties of the moment, was published with Churchill's tribute as a foreword. 'Had he achieved nothing more than the example he has set us of unselfish courage and constancy in the support of what he deemed the honour and interest of his fellow-countrymen, it would be enough,' wrote Churchill. 'But the distressed of the whole world have learnt to look to him and through him to Parliament for a patient hearing and the redress of wrongs.'

As soon as the Home Guard, then under its first name of Local Defence Volunteers, was initiated he hurried to enlist. He was the first M.P. to get his armlet. Armlets were for some time all that the L.D.V. did get. Old enmities were buried in the exhilaration of present danger and sacrifice. He found himself on terms of the warmest brotherhood with ex-appeasers, with ex-pacifists, even with Papists, as they learnt to handle their rifles on the terrace of the House. I asked myself to lunch one spring day. He replied with his usual laconic postcard, 'One o'clock, on the Terrace or in the ruins.' That night the Palace of Westminster was hit. 'You can't go in,' said the policeman on duty, at five-to-one. 'It's been hit.' 'Oh, but I must,' I argued, 'it's to meet Colonel Wedgwood and I'm sure he'll be where he said.' At that moment he appeared, to bear out my claim.

It was small wonder that he ended his autobiography with the words:

As for the time in which we live — Is not England at last taking its proper place, sacrificing all, standing alone against

234

evil? Alone in arms, but backed by the prayers and carrying the hopes of all the peoples of the world. Few would not find it exhilarating thus to stand armed in the last ditch with good comrades in so righteous a cause.

'*To be concluded, sometime, somewhere.*' So he broke off in 1940 and it fell to me to conclude. There were still some troubles and disappointments to come. The fight for the rights of refugees was continuous. The wholesale internment of the summer of 1940 sent him to hammer on the doors of the Home Office with an armful of individual cases and to raise the question of principle repeatedly in Parliament and the Press. In an article in *Time and Tide* that autumn he suggested the formation of a European Legion, an organization to make. the best use of the mental and physical resources of refugees, whether in a civil or military capacity against Hitler. On a narrower front he still carried on his fight for refugee Jews to be allowed to bear arms instead of being confined to the functions of the Pioneer Corps.

One refugee, a young girl named Leonora Bendit, ardently anxious to serve the cause of freedom, wrote him letters of such vehemence that he pictured her as a modern Valkyrie. When she arrived for an interview he was nonplussed to find her small, svelte and even shy. But her spirit was stout enough. It was partly as a result of his talk with her that he began an agitation — which was ultimately successful — for the enlistment of refugees in the A.T.S., where some of them did very well.

In the summer of 1941 he sailed for America, chiefly to speak for Zionism but no doubt he was also hoping to do as much as he had done in the previous war to bring America in on the side of democracy. For what the United States had already done and was doing for children evacuated from Great Britain he felt a profound gratitude which he expressed in the warmest terms on all occasions. He certainly also looked on this journey as an opportunity for giving thanks in person for 'the limitless generosity of the American people'.

The *Staffordshire Evening Sentinel*, in whose pages he was by now an institution, was moved to celebrate his departure in verses beginning:

> From Europe's last bastion of freedom we send
> To God's country of promise, the underdog's friend;
> Whom the world disinherits, their battle he shares,
> Though his only reward is a place in their prayers.

The tour began well enough and he spoke on Zionism to large and friendly audiences, but he had a bad heart attack in New Jersey and was hurried away to the Jewish hospital. Flowers poured in like a waterfall and none of the doctors would take any fees, but he had to give up lecturing. The end of the tour was utterly darkened by a campaign against him in the isolationist Press. He next projected a tour of Australia to speak on the war, but the cautious authorities, afraid of what he might say on the Palestine and refugee questions, would not authorize it.

VI

In the New Year Honours of 1942 he was raised to the peerage. In spite of the hard things he had said about the House of Lords in the past he was delighted; his new dignity appealed to his sense of history, and he enjoyed choosing supporters for his coat-of-arms.

I have chosen white lions with forked tails holding a ragged staff [he wrote to Ralph]. The staff is the emblem of our ancestor the King-maker; the lions are the arms of the father of that Parliament (Simon de Montfort), of which I am the most dutiful son. This touch of insolent assumption pleases me. Till Hitler invades us I shall remain your live and kicking brother Jos.

Besides he felt that he was growing old and looked forward to a quieter life in the Lords. 'I am looking forward to a more unmuzzled friendlier platform,' he wrote to Camilla, 'made of humanitarian planks and free from constituency calls.' But he was anxious that old friends on the Left should not disapprove. His wife wavered a little between the charm of the new idea and old egalitarian principles, but, as he told Camilla in another letter, 'she is almost reconciled to it because her aunts will like it. There never was anyone less of a snob than your step-mother'. A letter he wrote in answer to congratulations from a staunch friend of old Land Song days expresses what he felt:

My dear Campion,

The honour would not have been complete without this perfect letter from you. Only yesterday I was thinking a little sadly that my most constant friend in politics for 37 years might disapprove. And today I get a letter to keep for the rest of my days. You have warmed my heart and I think that is the thanks you would like best.

His year in the Lords gave him some satisfaction. He found in that House a more courteous audience and the manner of procedure was less exacting than that in the Commons. He described it to his daughter Camilla as the 'apotheosis of the perfect Christian life, a complete anarchy where each makes his own rules and is guided by his own good taste'.

Yet quite soon he was trying to get the rules altered.

Since law lords may subsequently be called on to give judgments arising out of legislation, it is understood that they do not intervene in debates on highly controversial bills lest the impartiality of their opinions might later be suspect. The measures from the discussions of which they will refrain are indicated by the Chancellor. Josiah was very soon approaching his old friend Lord Macmillan to suggest that the law lords should on occasion depart from this practice. Lord Macmillan put the arguments for adhering to it, to which Josiah soon returned a characteristic reply:

I do not wish you 'to blow off in a controversial spirit about all and sundry' but to explain, advise and guide public opinion. The House of Lords has a great future in moral leadership. Public opinion can be more powerful than police and is a better indicator as we become more responsive to freedom.

I do not want anybody to 'blow off in a controversial spirit' but I do want Parliament to fulfil its proper function of government through reason and argument and conviction of justice. In a sense that is controversy. But the controversy we all should avoid is partisanship and all the cases to which Simon refers were of that description of party warfare which may well be the Achilles heel of democracy.

I want both judges and bishops to do their duty by their country as leaders and not as servants.

Meanwhile, 1942, that terrible year, ran its course. When the news was too bad and he lay long awake at night he went back to his History and spent the small hours correcting details in his fifteenth-century Parliamentary biographies. He found in the disasters of the past an anodyne against Tobruk and Singapore. 'Disaster is not disgrace' he wrote to Camilla.

At about this time he began to realize the painful

problem which would soon lie before the libertarian Left. He had recently delivered at a somewhat Right Wing public meeting an excoriating attack on the rules and regulations embodied in the proposed Town and Country Planning Act. To his younger brother Ralph he wrote, 'that audience liked it too much and made me feel a bit guilty'. He did not live to face the uncomfortable dilemma of the Progressive who finds his views suddenly popular among the Reactionaries. He did, however, in his *Testament to Democracy* make clear his objection to the legislative increase of regulations of all kinds. The danger, as he still saw it, came from the well-meant interference of private bodies whose plans for the improvement of mankind were in earlier times usually embodied in Private Members bills. Of these he wrote:

There must be fifty societies of this sort who have a bill ready, to improve the world and assist their members. All are well intentioned; but I regret to say that most of their bills involve putting into prison some innocent person — innocent, that is, until the bill becomes an Act of Parliament.

Few notice this penal clause, so intent are they on 'doing good'. I always attend with pleasure on those Friday afternoons, when both sides chorus approval of some impertinent bill, in order maliciously to puncture the bubble of benevolence. The Society for the Prevention of Cruelty to Animals is one which all should support. They have a bill for the licensing and inspecting of livery stables to prevent 'crocks' being hired out for butchers to ride. Ninety-nine out of a hundred would vote for it blindfold. Why not?

Or the bill is to raise the age of consent. Why not?

Or to license dentists, or nurses, or architects, or shoe-blacks when there were any. Why not?

Or the bill is to limit interest demanded by moneylenders; or to prevent 'knock-out' sales; or to disinfect prostitutes; or to compel canal bargees to send their children to school;

to close shops on Sunday; or to stop fools from being fleeced.

I would undertake to make out a case for each and all of these bills which should move the House. Only — are you justified in sending an unlicensed man, or boy, or girl, to gaol in the sacred 'interests of society'? Are you justified in closing professions to the poor, in the interests of those already in the profession? Are you justified in raising the cost to the consumer? Are you justified in smashing a man whose business was legal, even useful, possibly honourable? I do not know; may be you are. But before an amiable majority, on a Friday afternoon (or any majority at any time), decides that you should do so, let them be asked to reflect that expediency and emotion are poor guides, that the individual 'has certain inalienable rights', and that every political crime, including the crucifixion, has been in accord with the will of a majority.

He does not appear to have contemplated that the State would before long take over this legislation and in such bulk that Private Members' time and bills would virtually disappear. Radical, and in that sense Left Wing, he emphatically was and grew more so with the years, but all the time he was shedding those very beliefs in State intervention which were becoming the hall-mark of the twentieth-century Left. In 1911 he had even himself introduced a measure making a certain act illegal — namely the giving of alcohol to a child under five. Would he have fathered such a measure in 1940? I very much doubt it.

Of the achievements of his youth, this was not one that he frequently recalled. But he was justly proud of his part in establishing a sound system of land valuation in Nigeria in 1912. When he looked back, he always felt that Socialism had taken a wrong turning when it parted company with Henry George, and in his latest speeches he was still preaching the good old cause. 'Town planning,' he said in November

1942 'is worth nothing and country planning is worth nothing unless you face up to the fact that your first and final duty is to throw open the land of England to the people of England so that they can work it and develop it.'

He still found much comfort in thinking of his family and of a now rapidly multiplying younger generation. As he wrote to Ralph

> We elders can sing *Nunc dimittis* with perfect confidence that there will be no dimming of the light. Also that our father and mother did their job well.
>
> Arrogantly yours Wedgwood.

As he approached the term of his journey he was feeling happier about the faith of his beloved country. He cared deeply about the English Church, although in the expressive phrase of the Bishop of Lichfield, 'he was a very unorthodox Christian, he sat loose to creeds and Churches'. But he loved the Church as a part of the shape and spirit of England and the advent of the wise and liberal Archbishop Temple — 'our perfect Archbishop', he wrote — gave him great comfort. Born in a strongly rationalist generation, he was not himself by instinct and feeling a rationalist. In a moment of self-revelation he wrote to Florence, 'I am a frightfully religious person. You may not have observed it but it is ludicrously true'. His kind of character is indeed hardly to be imagined without the strength of a powerful, if rather undefined, faith.

He certainly derived much happiness in his last years from his warm friendship with Edward Woods who became Bishop of Lichfield in 1937. In him he found a churchman whose unaffected goodness and profound charity were wholly after his own heart. The sentiment was reciprocated and a letter from the

Bishop written after an evening spent together is perhaps the best summing up that can be given on this point.

My dear Jos,

It was a real joy to be with you and your dear wife the other night. Most refreshing. You are a man after my own heart indeed, and I rejoice wholeheartedly in all the splendid things you do for the Kingdom of God. I dare say you wouldn't phrase it like that, but that is in fact, whatever you call it, the true objective of your efforts.

His chief anxiety to the end was the state of Palestine. Here he felt the policy of his country was unworthy of the cause for which the war was being fought or of her past standards. What he had seen and heard convinced him of the strongly pro-Arab sympathies of the administration and the anti-Semitic prejudice of the Palestine police and he was deeply distressed and indignant at the unwillingness of the Colonial Office to inquire thoroughly into the question. 'What we want in the public service,' he declared in the House of Lords, 'is not that things should be kept dark for the honour of the department, but that things should be kept correct for the honour of the country.' This was the occasion of that bitter exchange with Lord Cranborne described in the previous chapter. Lord Cranborne called his allegations 'unbridled, reckless and . . . calculated to do a great deal of serious harm'. Josiah was already very ill although he held his own vigorously in that debate. A few weeks later, almost the last time he spoke in the House, he reverted to the occasion: 'I have no objection to acquiring a reputation in your Lordships' House for saying things which may appear indiscreet when I think they should be said in the free Parliament of a free country.'

His time for saying them was fast running out. That winter (1942-43), his old friend Charles Buxton died, another staunch champion of the oppressed. Who would defend causes now? he wrote to Camilla, 'Charlie Buxton is dead, Noel temporarily blind and I'm not feeling too well myself.' A few days later he had the heart attack from which he never fully recovered.

He struggled valiantly to live on, and sometimes seemed to rally almost towards convalescence, but much of the time he was under morphia. He passed his days, when he was well enough to read or think, checking up minor errors in his History of Parliament, or working out a new kind of family tree. He was embowered in flowers, the most splendid of which, all in valiant colours, Churchill had even in the anxiety of that spring of 1943 found time to send him. Once when I was with him he was talking — but a long way off — about the advance of racialism in Africa; he was at that moment beyond hearing any argument even if a soothing one could have been found. I could only hold his hand and hope that soon the exhausted brain would wander on to some happier theme. To his wife and to those of his children who were with him, this heart-rending experience must have happened very often. Sometimes it was possible to make a little conversation. A week or two before he died he asked me what I was writing. I told him that I was trying to put together a biography of William the Silent. Recollections of Motley flooded into his mind from his boyhood; for a second his eyes almost lit up. 'A good subject,' he said, 'those are . . . those are the things to write about . . .' his voice faded again.

Sometimes, to some very old and dear friend, he managed to write a note. Dr. George Gooch has sent

me what must have been one of the last from his hand.
It has all the old courtesy and bravura:

Thank you for 35 years of example and help. Others
will come on in our place but none that loved and trusted
so well.

Jos.

I may survive, but it wants saying.

This was written on July 6th. He died on July 26th,
1943, as Italian Fascism collapsed and Mussolini fled.
The news came an hour too late for him to know.

VII

He had once suggested that if anyone wrote his
life it should be called *The Last of the Radicals* and
should be 'a clarion call against the constructors of a
safe and unjust society'. Twice during the last
months he had spoken his own epitaph. Once, when
a fellow firewatcher asked him to autograph a book,
he wrote in it, 'To a firewatcher from an incendiary.'
A little later when Lord Cranborne, over the Palestine
Question, accused him of inciting to violence, he
declared, 'my whole life has been an incitement to
violence'.

A passionate love of justice and a contempt for
caution — these were the strongest forces in his
character. Tell him a course was expedient and he
suspected it, and you, at once. He did not rebutt the
charge of incendiarism or of indiscretion; he did not
rebutt the charge of irresponsibility. He believed that
these things might be, often were, the duty of the good
man. The great administrators, the great architects of
a state are not made of such stuff. It is questionable

even if great leaders can be, for if the capacity to take risks is necessary in leadership, the fervour which will take *all* risks may dangerously lose what has been dangerously won. But the man who will take all risks, the man who will never consider any other aspect of the question save that of justice is essential to society. In an old and cautious society such men are rare and precious.

This was the significance of his career, this the value of his life to the country of which he was so critical and so proud.

He had died in London, but he was buried in the village where he had been born, at Barlaston, in North Staffordshire.

The main line to Manchester goes through this station, and it was there that, by arrangement, the express halted on the brilliant July day, and three generations of family climbed out on to the platform, while all the occupants of the train began to stare out of the open windows to see why the train was stopping, and remained to watch in silence. The coffin could hardly be seen for the flowers and everyone who knew him had had the same idea, for, piled in massive splendour in the relentless sun, were the gold and red and flame colour of high summer, rich and glorious and living.

The service was in the little church which he had attended as a child. My father read the lesson:

I have fought a good fight; I have finished my course; I have kept the faith.

INDEX

INDEX

249

INDEX

250

INDEX

INDEX